CONFRONTATION IN ADOLESCENCE

CONFRONTATION IN
ADOLESCENCE

JACK L. FADELY, Ed.D.

Educational Psychology Department,
Butler University,
Indianapolis, Indiana

VIRGINIA N. HOSLER, B.S., M.S.

Special Education,
Peoria Public Schools,
Peoria, Illinois

The C. V. Mosby Company

ST. LOUIS • TORONTO • LONDON 1979

Copyright © 1979 by The C. V. Mosby Company

All rights reserved. No part of this book may be reproduced
in any manner without written permission of the publisher.

Printed in the United States of America

The C. V. Mosby Company
11830 Westline Industrial Drive, St. Louis, Missouri 63141

Library of Congress Cataloging in Publication Data

Fadely, Jack L   , 1934-
   Confrontation in adolescence.

   Bibliography: p.
   Includes index.
   1. Adolescence. 2. Adolescent psychology.
3. Juvenile delinquency. I. Hosler, Virginia Neemes,
1943-   joint author. II. Title.
HQ796.F28   364.36   78-6709
ISBN 0-8016-1553-4

GW/M/M 9 8 7 6 5 4 3 2 1

FOREWORD

Adolescence was a time when all of us were searching for acceptance by others and personal responsibility for our own lives. Society thereby obligates itself to equip young people with the means—the educational, social, and cultural background, the personal and economic security—to understand and accept responsibility. Clearly it is to our children, the nation's future, that we must give direction and assistance. Direction and assistance cannot be provided without understanding the many turmoils taking place within the life of the youngster.

Law enforcement officers interact with juveniles on a daily basis in the normal course of their work. In order to make these encounters more positive and meaningful for both sides, the officer needs to have a basic understanding of adolescents: basic knowledge concerning their development and growth. Adolescence is a special stage of human growth and development. This particular stage has been viewed as a most conflict- and confusion-ridden part of life. Without a feeling for what an adolescent is experiencing during this period, an officer cannot approach and deal with the young person as effectively as might be possible.

Law enforcement officers traditionally are employed, trained, and directed to find the answers to the questions of "what, who, where, when, and how." They have been generally aware of some of the primary factors that contribute to produce criminal behavior, and have not been basically concerned with the "why" of human behavior. This book sheds light on the "why" of adolescent behavior and offers sound ideas and guidelines concerning more skillful ways to deal with troubled youth. The formation years of human development during adolescence have often been misunderstood because of the erroneous assumption that we do understand this troublesome time because we ourselves have come through this period.

Fadely and Hosler present an easily followed and practical description of the nature and path of adolescent behavior development. The physical, emotional, intellectual, and social changes accompanying adolescence are discussed. The adolescent reacts to these changes, and, in turn, society reacts to the behavior of the adolescent. In this book are realistic guidelines concerning how law enforcement can more skillfully deal with youth and maintain objectivity.

The information this book offers is relevant not only to law enforcement officers, but also to educators, parents, social workers, as well as the entire criminal justice field. All of these are enforcers of norms, rules, and so forth, and need to understand adolescent development. Juvenile delinquency is an increasing problem for America. Citizens are concerned about the need for more control and for preventive measures. This resource book will serve to give direction and advice for parents, schools, and other child-caring agencies.

Alfred R. Bennett

Executive Director, Indiana Youth Authority,
Indiana Department of Corrections,
Indianapolis, Indiana

PREFACE

There are many books on juvenile delinquency that provide a great deal of theory along with a small amount of practical information about the juvenile offender. In the early morning hours, in some lonely section of the city, or on a country road, such books seem far away and of little help. A law enforcement officer, aside from attempting to live down the image of the "tough guy hassling kids," is often overcome with feelings of helplessness and confusion when faced with the task of questioning a group of adolescents who may be breaking the law or testing the limits of society's rules.

One of the deficiencies in training programs for juvenile officers has been educating them in adolescent psychology. Understanding the nature of adolescence and the ability to use that understanding in law enforcement are essential to officer training. This brief book is written for those who must deal with the specific problems of the adolescent offender. Dealing with young offenders is a difficult job that carries little satisfaction from merely enforcing the law. In the first place, law enforcement officers are human beings—people with humane feelings who sincerely want to do a good job. They may have youngsters of their own at home and have some reservations about dealing harshly with young people not unlike their own children. In addition, the experienced officer who is well aware of the consequences of criminal behavior will want to spend some extra effort in assisting the juvenile.

The material for this book was developed through interviews with law enforcement officers and through participation in intervention programs for delinquent youths in juvenile centers and correctional institutions. We directed training programs in understanding adolescence with police officers, security officers, correctional workers, and professional counselors, and spent innumerable hours counseling parents of troubled adolescents. These experiences, along with our training in adolescent development, led to the realization that while criminal justice workers often understood the law, they did not understand the nature of adolescence. In many individual cases it was clear that specialists in development understood adolescent development just as criminal justice workers understood the law. But there were few individuals in either profession who considered the relationship between the normal aspects of adolescent development and inherent possibilities for confrontation between the adolescent and the law. These confrontations, it seems, often depend as much on the nature of adolescence itself as they do on the larger issues of cultural deprivation, physiological problems, or social deviancy. This book is an attempt to show how adolescent development may contribute to many forms of delinquent behavior. It is hoped that law enforcement officials will be able to separate those adolescents caught up in their normal stage of life from those who display some form of deviance requiring legal or mental health intervention, thus giving more strength to prevention of crime.

Adolescent crimes have increased significantly in recent years, and special branches of law enforcement have been developed to deal with the causes of this increase. Although many problems and techniques are similar in other areas of law enforcement, juvenile law has unique characteristics. Adolescents are much less capable of recognizing the consequences of their behavior than adults, and their actions may leave more questions concerning actual criminality than may the actions of adults. Crucial to the adolescent challenge are questions of what constitutes appropriate adolescent behavior and how one may help youngsters and their parents with their problems. Adolescence is one of the most confusing and emotionally explosive periods of life. This is easy to forget with age and is easier to forget when one is confronted with an adolescent who is negative and challenging. It is the responsibility of the adult to understand the situation and maintain a cool head.

In reviewing delinquency, Cressey and Ward state:

> Perhaps it shows, also, that police more readily select for official action those juveniles whose appearance and demeanor make it easy to conclude that they (the juveniles) have withdrawn their consent to be governed.*

Cressey and Ward suggest that police officers are more selective in their action to those juveniles who appear delinquent than they are about the actions of juveniles.

Although preconceptual bias operates in us all according to our own experience and beliefs, when we function in official or professional roles, we must add factual knowledge to our experience to assure that we no longer operate from the stance of prejudice. The police officer is an

---

*Cressey, Donald R., and Ward, David A.: Delinquency, crime and social process, New York, 1969, Harper & Row, Publishers, p. 123.

individual who is trained and charged with enforcement of the law, but enforcement cannot be exercised to the fullest extent of its protection of the individual if it is exercised in a biased manner. Enforcement of the law, as in pronouncement of sentence in the courtroom, is more than merely acting. It is a practice of considered interaction with members of the community at large. Interaction with juveniles requires more than enforcement; it requires an understanding of the nature of the juvenile mind, of the inherent conflict of the adolescent state itself, and of the difficulties that are experienced as we emerge from one psychological state to another. The police officer, burdened with the tremendous responsibility required to effectively enforce the law, often knows too little about the nature of the individuals who are the recipients of enforcement.

This book is a resource for officers concerning many of the normal aspects of adolescent development. It is not intended as a handbook on how to enforce the law concerning juveniles. Training in law enforcement is left to the agency programs provided for law enforcement officials. We hope that this survey of adolescent development will provide additional information of value to the well-trained law enforcement officer.

Finally, this book should prove an important resource for other professionals working within the criminal justice system. Judges, probation officers, court workers, and lawyers will find in it information that will extend their understanding of the adolescent who needs assistance in his dilemma. It will also be an important resource for teachers, counselors, and cottage unit or correctional officers working in juvenile institutions or centers.

We express our appreciation to all who have assisted in the preparation of this book. In particular, we wish to acknowledge helpful suggestions received from Lt. Dunlevey of the Peoria Police Department, Rick Williams from the Gift Avenue Home for Delinquent Youth, and Trooper Wamsley from the Illinois State Police Department. We thank Dr. Clemens Bartollas of Sagamon State University for reviewing and making helpful recommendations for modifying the manuscript. We also wish to thank Sonna Aden for her continued patience and assistance in editing the text, and Don Kamoss for the line drawings, which are adaptations of illustrations that appear in the journal *American Education* and in Diane Papalia and Sally Wendkos Olds's book *A Child's World*. Sharon Dorsey and Pat Porter were helpful in their assistance with typing. From countless sources have come ideas and suggestions that find their expression in this book.

Jack L. Fadely
Virginia N. Hosler

CONTENTS

CONFRONTATION IN ADOLESCENCE

CHAPTER 1

AN OVERVIEW OF ADOLESCENCE

Even if I knew who I was,
I am not sure I would like it.

Adolescence as a physical and emotional stage has always existed; we have only recently recognized it as a separate stage deserving and requiring separate study. At one time individuals went from childhood into adulthood with no transitional period between. When children reached the age of 12 or 14, they were expected to assume a contributory role in the work of the family. Shortly thereafter, marriage was either expected or arranged. But as society developed technologically, a transitional period was established that served to prepare the individual for an occupation and for family responsibilities. As technology advances, there is an increasing tendency to extend this period of preparation and education before the individual assumes full responsibility as a member of the community. There is little doubt that the pace and complexity of today's world demand far more education than was necessary 30 or 40 years ago, and many young people choose longer periods of career preparation over early marriage. These changes have significantly affected the adolescent period. More adolescents than in the past are apt to view the years between 14 and 20 as years of education and personal growth. Economic realities have also tended to extend the period between childhood and adulthood, when the individual assumes a family or community responsibility.

Adolescence is generally considered to be that period between 13 and 18 years of age. Some professionals in human growth designate the ages between 12 and 14 as a period of preadolescence, with adolescence being that period between 14 and 18. However, because of the tremendous maturational variability of individuals within any group of adolescents, it is difficult to say when adolescence begins and ends chronologically. There are many psychological and social levels of maturation that may not be achieved by all individuals at the same age. Thus, the designation of the adolescent period is as much an economic and social concept as it is a reality in human development. Many law enforcement officers meet adults who possess certain characteristics of adolescence. There are also individuals who appear to be quite mature long before the ages of 18 or 21 years. Milestones of personal development that can be observed and measured indicate a stage of maturation regardless of the individual's age; we cannot assume that an individual who is 15 or 30 has in fact all the specific psychological capabilities expected at that age. We must look at the nature of adolescent development and at the individual's behavior in order to truly understand his needs and problems, rather than expect his age alone to indicate his level of maturity.

THE QUIET BEFORE THE STORM

The period of development from around 6 or 7 years through 12 years of age is called middle and late childhood. For the child, the years in elementary school are somewhat tranquil compared with the emotional turmoil of adolescence. In fact, these years preceding adolescence are sometimes referred to as the latency period, usually in regard to sexual development. During this period the child not only appears to be unaware of sexual aspects of human behavior but also does not display many physical characteristics related to sexual development. At this time the child is growing rapidly in size, coordination, physical endurance, and in mental or intellectual areas. This period of relative quiet is characterized by the child's development of physical and mental skills and is not usually marked by any great personal crisis or stress. Late childhood, with its freedom from stress and from adult responsibilities, offers a rare security: structure and direction of parents and teachers, rules that are fairly clear, and a direction well set by learning tasks that occupy much of the time. This is not so for adolescence; therefore, childhood is often referred to as "the quiet before the storm." At about the age of 14, the individual enters a period of tremendous physical, emotional, intellectual, and social change.

THE IDENTITY CRISIS IN ADOLESCENCE

During early to middle childhood, the child grows rapidly and establishes his basic self-concept and a value system that will carry him until preadolescence. In adolescence the child becomes a young adult, and self-concept issues again become significant to his maturation.

The first and major crisis in adolescence is an identity crisis. It is based on the psychosexual changes experienced in adolescence and forces personal awareness to be focused on self-identity. Sexual growth accelerates with the production of sex-related hormones, producing all of the secondary sexual characteristics of adulthood, including pubic hair, facial hair, change in voice tone, breasts, and alterations in general physical structure relative to male and female characteristics. All these physical changes are accompanied by social and psychological changes. The time will vary with individuals, but at approximately 12 years of age, because of the social station provided by emergence from elementary school into middle school and high school, all children are forced to an awareness of sexuality, particularly their own. With the interaction of these social and psychological factors, children enter adolescence. The personal trials and problems both boys and girls experience at the onset of adolescence and how these problems are modulated by the child, his family, and his school determine how well adolescent development will proceed.

SEXUAL STEREOTYPES

Children become aware of how they should be through television, books, peers, and family life styles. There are sexual stereotypes to which most men and women are expected to adhere, although varying life styles of parents and peer groups can alter these stereotypes to some degree. The following are the general sexual stereotypes that appear throughout the culture:

Men	Women
Aggressive	Passive
Dominant	Submissive
Tough-minded	Tender-minded
Adventuresome	Cautious
Strong and athletic	Attractive
Realistic and practial	Illogical and emotional
Competitive	Cooperative

These are not all the possible characteristics that are attributed to men and women in the culture, but they are typical of the most widespread sexual stereotypes. We may take issue with such stereotypes and resist their injustices and inappropriateness. In recent years there have been efforts to change these stereotypes through women's liberation, inclusion of women in athletics, opening new occupations for women, and special-group propaganda. However, the basic stereotypes appear strongly resistant to such agents of change.

Our experience has been that today's youth more often demonstrate these stereotyped characteristics of men and women than any major change in their social conditioning or their behavior. This is not to say that this condition is good or bad but simply that, despite all our intellectual, political, and social efforts, young people are still submitted to the traditional socialization according to sex, and they reflect this conditioning in their general behavioral interactions and values. In spite of some exceptions in public programs and in basic family patterns, it is safe to say that the basic stereotypes still exist and have tremendous impact on how the adolescent views himself. For the courts and the police officer, what is presently true is more important than what might be sociologically desired.

THE ADOLESCENT BOY

In peer groups of boys, it is apparent that the athletic and dominant boy is held as the ideal model. Most boys compare themselves with this model, and positive or negative feelings result. For most boys the emergence of masculine physical characteristics is both an exciting and embarrassing experience. At this stage most boys will tend to take risks to prove how strong or courageous they are. If they are unable to take the lead, they will attempt to join a peer group in which there are strong models to emulate. Thus is formed the first strong male bonding in which boys begin to identify with other boys. For the male adolescent, possibly because of his expected role of dominance, there often appears to be a stronger need to display strength and personal competence than there is for the female adolescent. Thus, boys may be propelled into group association in order to assure themselves of their capabilities. Perhaps for this reason a boy's effeminate behavior may be viewed so much more critically by other boys than a girl's masculinity is viewed by other girls. The sexual stereotype for boys may become more critical for the male adolescent. A fear of failure to fulfill the masculine role causes anxiety and subsequent aggression. Performance becomes a test of manhood, whether in the bedroom or on the football field.

There are, then, two major criteria for the measurement of emerging manhood: The boy must demonstrate *belonging capabilities* to the group, and he must perform feats that indicate his adequacy as a boy or, ideally, as a man. Through belonging to an appropriate male group and through performance, the boy develops a self-identity that is, according to what he has been told and shown, appropriate for a man. In this way he becomes a man in his own mind and in the perception of those around him. What are some of the general expectations held in our culture for the male adult which the adolescent must now begin to live up to?

The following statements are recognizable as part of the general mythology of manhood:

1. Men don't cry.
2. Men are strong and take their part in fights.
3. Men make the decisions and are responsible for taking care of women.
4. Men are tough and never act like sissies.
5. Really capable men take over in sexual acts, and women like to make love to strong, aggressive men.
6. All girls like to go to bed, but they often act like they don't.
7. Men who "make it" with girls are the most popular.
8. Nice girls don't like to "get it on," so you have to find those girls who do. But of course you wouldn't want to marry one.
9. The bigger your penis, the better. In fact, how much of a man you is pretty much determined by how big you are.
10. If you have never been to bed with a girl, you haven't grown up.
11. Women admire men who are strong.
12. Men are smarter than women.

Our sophisticated technological culture has come a long way toward breaking down and changing these stereotypes, but there are still many boys who adhere to them. Even in more enlightened families, boys are still subtly indoctrinated with such concepts. The training of the boy for his dominant role in society is accompanied by a consonant biological tendency. There are some indications that male hormones do tend to

5

produce individuals who are more aggressive, explosive, and competitive. Thus, despite cultural changes in the stereotypes, there is a tremendous social and biological tendency for the masculine stereotype to be actualized. Law enforcement officers often find that the most aggressive crimes involve boys. Although there has been a tremendous increase in violent and aggressive crimes committed by women, there is little doubt that the aggressive syndrome of adolescent development still belongs to the male adolescent. More important, it must be realized that the aggressive and competitive drive is a normal part of adolescent growth.

The adolescent boy is concerned with his identity, and that identity involves the establishment of the male stereotype. The group-belonging tendency forces the growing boy into behavior that, although important in initial identity, will not usually endure into adulthood. The aggressive and adventuresome period lasts until the boy reaches several important milestones in individual growth. These behaviors usually must be worked through toward the establishment of a healthy self-concept. When a boy has established his identity and can feel secure, then the most energized aspect of his maleness subsides into a more confident and individualistic style. This behavior identifies him not only with his group but, more important, as an individual within that group. Once this level of growth has been achieved, the boy is free to look toward more important aspects of development.

A second major and critical developmental stage in the identity crisis is that of emergence from the family identity. Throughout childhood, the boy holds the same values and general beliefs as the family. If his final separation and establishment of personal identity are to occur, he will have to become distinct in his own values, apart and different from the historical pattern of his family. This is critical, for without this development he may be tied to the authority and identity of his father and mother and siblings. Thus, a major crisis for many parents is the sometimes surprising rebellion that boys will display within a family where there has never been any sort of difficulties. Suddenly, the boy announces that he will not attend church, or he selects friends that he knows will cause family disapproval. He may begin to engage in activities that have been generally unacceptable to the family. He may abandon former academic goals or discontinue activities in which he has been involved for some time. Often he feels as confused about his behavior as his parents, but he feels a tremendous need to alter his general life style, interests, and values. This need, of course, is part of developing an identity distinct from his history and family. The effort to express a new and emerging personality often takes the boy far away from his basic family value structure. The family may respond with confusion, hostility, anger, and eventually tremendous resistance to his emerging independence.

6

This period of development is met in different ways by both families and boys. Some families who are very supportive of children making their own decisions, while providing definite parental guidance and setting limits, find that their sons develop through this stage without tremendous difficulties. However, there are so many factors involved that even effective parents may find themselves at odds with their own child. Not understanding all factors, they react initially with pleading and reasoning and finally with confusion and hostility.

If the boy has experienced success in school through academic achievement, sports, school activities, or in work efforts, his energies may be focused on continuing down already existent avenues for expressing his individuality and male assertiveness. In such cases the family can be very supportive of his activities, and his behavior fits into the acceptable mode of adolescent behavior. This is the general rule; however, there are significant numbers of boys in school who have never found adequate success in any of these traditional outlets. In these cases the boys may turn to more negative or unacceptable activities and peers in order to work through this initial identity crisis without the support of parents and school. Society and school reward the winners and punish the losers. Since only a few individuals can win by making the sports team, achieving high grades, or gaining social recognition, many boys are left to forge for themselves some means of establishing their manhood. The automobile has been one effective and accessible means. With the automobile the adolescent boy can gain status, developing it into a machine of great power. He can use it to obtain dates and to travel far from the eyes of his family and school peers with whom he has little status.

The automobile and the adolescent

The automobile has a highly significant symbolism for the adolescent, particularly in the American culture. Besides the identification of power and status that the automobile gives the adolescent, it provides a concrete representation of independence. It is, after all, the establishment of independence that is one of the major goals of adolescence. The mobility provided by the automobile erodes the control of parents and increases the opportunity for the adolescent to act out his own impulses without the proximity of parental guidance and evaluation. Thus, the automobile can accelerate the adolescent's freedom and independence from parental authority, even though this may last only for a few hours each day before he must return home. Furthermore, the automobile allows for wish fulfillment in the form of attaining those things associated with the automobile. The association of power and status with the automobile is well outlined in the media, where the automobile becomes the means of projecting the individual's personality and ego identification. For the adolescent the ego involvement with his "wheels" can become extensive and an overstatement of what the automobile represents for much of society. The automobile can be altered to reflect rebellion, aggression, adventure, and challenge through the many accessories and modifications that give the appearance of power and status.

In many subcultures automobiles are decorated as a means of displaying not only status and power but also sexual symbolism, through gaudy painting, plush interiors, and vivid colors, all of which reflect internal emotional states. This decoration is a means of externalizing personal needs. The adolescent often becomes absorbed to the extent that the automobile becomes, in psychological terms, an ego extension: I am what my car is; my car is not only me but represents me.

In the forests each spring the males of many wild animal species prepare horns, teeth, claws, and wings for mating battles. On city streets and country roads adolescent boys prepare their weapons of the mating ritual in the form of automobiles. The power, speed, and maneuverability of the automobile becomes the means of challenge to other boys in the forest of city and country streets and roads. All that is required for a test of manhood is the accidental appearance of another auto next to yours at a stoplight, coming onto the highway at an interchange, or leaving the parking lot of a local hangout. The ensuing challenge and drag down a street are as predictable as the adolescent state itself. The auto becomes a weapon, a means of doing battle and testing one's emerging manhood.

Adolescents will often become so immersed in the power of and ego identification with their automobiles that they will respond in inappropriate ways. Intervention in the adolescent's behavior while he is in his automobile can provoke responses in the adolescent that are uncharacteristic of his behavior under other circumstances. For example, many normal adolescents may be usually somewhat law abiding but, in the thrill of late-night escapades and challenges from other adolescents, may temporarily become less than law abiding and even pseudodelinquent. The adolescent will act out impulses that he usually is able to hold in check. Confrontation with the law at this time can propel the adolescent into risk-taking behaviors of which he is usually incapable. For this reason the adolescent who faces the officer with his parents in the courtroom is frequently quite different from the adolescent who confronted the officer in a 10-mile chase a few nights before.

For the adolescent who is alienated from the culture, the automobile and all of its attendant psychological characteristics can become a distorted, disturbed representation of his anger, frustration, and hostility. For this adolescent or group of adolescents, the automobile can become so significant that they will steal one and engage in criminal acts. Thus, it becomes both a mechanical and a psychological vehicle of rebellion.

The automobile becomes something else that is extremely important in human behavior: symbolic territory. The adolescent feels ownership and psychological dominance when he is in his automobile. The adolescent who is confronted by a police officer while he remains in his automobile is much more likely to display aggression than is the adolescent who is removed from his automobile and sits in the squad car. Many police officers learn that less aggression will be shown by an individual who is in the police officer's automobile, or territory, than when the police officer attempts to confront the individual in his own car.

The adult and the adolescent

There is another cultural characteristic of boys growing into manhood that is particularly unsettling to the male adult. In all social groups of animals, the young constantly test their emerging strength and virility against the dominant males; adolescent boys are intrigued with testing the limits of the male adult. The boys will become the leaders and dominant individuals, taking the place of aging male adults in tomorrow's world. Many men find this particularly distressing and often respond with aggressive and challenging behaviors. Certainly the juvenile officer, although he is the mature adult, sometimes feels more sense of threat and aggression within himself when dealing with adolescent boys than otherwise might be felt.

The police officer must recognize this degree of normal aggressive challenge inherent in adolescent behavior if he is to effectively work with adolescents. Too often adults fail to realize that our aggressive response to adolescents may suggest a lack of maturity in our own development. The police officer represents to the adolescent the authority of parents, teachers, and the adult community in general. It is easier to act out toward a depersonalized representation of authority than it is to act out toward a personal authority figure with whom we have a relationship. Individuals can punish, threaten, and even kill others if they do not know them personally, as in war. But when we *know* someone, actual aggression or homicide is less likely. It is true that many homicides occur within family groups, but generally the emotional response to homicide is less in cases where we are acting out toward a stranger or someone with whom we have no relationship.

The police officer becomes not a person but a stranger who represents authority. The adolescent is more likely to confront the police officer in aggressive ways than a member of the school faculty or the family. Familiarity can often defuse aggression. This is why communication, talking, and relating to the adolescent during confrontation are so important. When an individual is forced to communicate, language becomes a substitute for physical aggression. This is the key, in human

9

culture, to the ability to defuse aggression and become socialized. Words, substituted for actual aggression, become the weapons of confrontation. Hopefully, the police officer learns early that aggression is not always the best approach to confrontation.

An adolescent boy finds himself in conflict with the law because of many normal adolescent needs. He is confused but feels impelled to follow through with his behavior. The law official, responsible for maintaining order and reason, is faced with a youth who is following normal but poorly directed patterns of behavior that the officer must redirect or stop. There are all of the ingredients for conflict between two opposing forces, neither of which is willing to give in. The boy loses his identity if he submits, while the adult loses his dignity and control, and perhaps his job, if he gives in.

It is here that the role of the police officer can become one of justice and education rather than merely enforcement. For example, the adolescent who is threatened by arrest or confrontation is likely to respond in a more dramatic and emotional manner than the police officer. Not only has the police officer had more experience and practice in the game of confrontation, he is able to think through the situation with many more variables in mind than the simple aim of obtaining submission from the adolescent. The adolescent, however, is more likely to respond with emotionality ranging from aggression to withdrawal and anxiety. Because he is under threat, he is more likely to fight or run, confront or withdraw, or attempt to deal with the situation in some manner other than with logic and reason. Although we all tend to become somewhat physiologically tense during confrontation, adults should be able to control the reaction more effectively than adolescents. Police brutality, although often overstated or even staged by organized groups, can in isolated cases represent an officer who "loses his cool" under the stress of a situation and responds much like the adolescent himself. This is unfortunate, but it is human and always a danger. Teachers, psychologists, social workers, judges, and other professionals who work with adolescents would be less than truthful if they did not admit that at some time in their career they lost their sense or reason and reacted in an aggressive and punitive manner toward adolescents who somehow touched something important in the adult's own psychological make-up. It takes seasoning as a police officer, as in any profession, to learn how to maintain objectivity and coolness under threat. However, no matter how effective we become, there may come that time when we find our limit, our special situation, in which we react in ways we would not normally. To deny this probability is to deny the reality of being human.

Understanding this, the adult should be able to modulate both his and the boy's behavior. If this occurs, then both individuals win, and the officer finds great satisfaction in providing an educational and supportive role that is preventive rather than punitive. If the behavior cannot be modulated, it is unlikely that either participant will emerge the winner. If the behaviors can be modulated, this is obviously the route that should be taken; otherwise, the law enforcement role is indicated.

Aggression and the adolescent

The identity crisis for boys initially involves being propelled into adolescence by both biological changes and social expectations that include the stereotyped male image. Although many adolescents enter and pass quietly through this initial phase, many do not. In the case of the latter, attempts to find some outlet for the need to demonstrate increased maturity lead them into unacceptable behavior.

In society, and particularly within the family, there is a subtle encouragement of aggression in boys that is not paralleled in the treatment of girls. The adolescent boy, in his dominant and socially perceived role as the aggressor, is usually given reinforcement for displaying conquests and novice behaviors that indicate he is beginning to assume his role as the sexual aggressor with the opposite sex. The father may display disapproval to his son and, at the same time, subtly encourage him to "like girls" and to display behaviors that indicate he is beginning to accept this role. For example, although boys are given curfew, many fathers take pride in their sons who break curfew while engaging in some behavior exhibiting male prowess. In essence, one should not break curfew, but, "What were you really doing with Betty?" There is a mixture of social indignation and a subtle wink and pat on the shoulder that indicates approval of male sexual prowess. This double message contains appropriate parental condemnation of breaking the rules but acceptance of appropriate sexual behaviors. If a boy is caught in "lovers' lane" in a compromising situation with Betty, he is, after all, under the protection of the belief that "boys will be boys," but Betty is often subject to less approval and acceptance. This sort of double standard creates much frustration when a teenage daughter begins to act more like a chip off the old masculine block than like the traditional passive and nurturing woman. Boys commit more crime; however, the societal stereotype encourages boys in behaviors that are more likely to result in some sort of offense. The trend today is that girls are also being encouraged by society to many of the same behaviors, and society and parents in particular are simply not ready for this.

Much has been said about the "generation gap." The term has many meanings and has been used to describe more difficulties between various age groups than the concept deserves. However, there is little doubt that federal laws concerning civil rights and women's rights, although

11

appropriate to our concepts of individual rights in a democracy, will take time for the population to accept. What most of us believe in theory we often do not accept in practice. We proclaim the rights of all individuals intellectually but are frequently unable to act out such beliefs if they threaten us specifically. Equal treatment of women in society relative to men is far from an accepted belief throughout the culture, although the courts have verified that it must be accepted under law, as in the case of racial equality. Those who benefit directly from the concept of equality are obviously most likely to be enthusiastic about the cause for equal rights. The teenage girl may accept these ideas and attempt to use their verification as a means to fulfill her own need to become free from authority. For the adolescent girl, already caught in a normal developmental period in which establishment of individuality is a major personal goal, legal and cultural emphasis on her right to be free and independent can enhance her own determination to establish independence. She can become, as women and girls could not so easily in the past, more determined about her independence and rights. Whereas the delinquent girl in the past might have continued to act out submissive and typically feminine roles, today she is more likely to identify with the whole women's rights movement and act out in more aggressive ways traditionally identified with boys.

People in our culture may accept women's rights in theory but often are unable to accept them in practice in their own life space. Thus, the adolescent girl runs headlong into a generation gap in which adults espouse equality for women while treating the girl in traditional ways within the family. To further complicate the issue, many mothers, themselves long held under the chauvinistic control of their spouses, subtly encourage their daughters' rebellion. However, once the daughter accepts her encouragement, the mother often finds herself unable to accept her daughter's confrontation. This phenomenon of societal encouragement of women's equality merging with typically adolescent needs for identity may be a significant factor in the increasing incorrigibility of many adolescent girls.

For the boy who has had an adequate amount of nurturing and support within the family and school during childhood, the temporary developmental difficulty of adolescence will usually give way to more subdued and appropriate behavior. However, for the boy who comes from a home in which family support has been poor and where economic and value structures have been atypical, this new phase of growth may continue to be expressed in deviant and hostile behaviors that lead to criminal involvement. In a particular situation, it is difficult to determine what factors are involved in the boy's history so that the officer can judge how to handle the situation. Following are some general guidelines that may be useful for both parents and juvenile officers in meeting aggressive behavior:

1. In confrontation with an aggressive adolescent, counteraggression is not indicated and often can stimulate more aggression on the part of the adolescent.

2. The adolescent who becomes assertive needs firm controls and definite limits to his behavior. These limits should be realistic and immediate. Many parents faced with a rebelling adolescent often either become too punitive, giving no room for the adolescent to maneuver in, or give in completely, hoping that he will "come to his senses." Both of these approaches end in frustration. Talking out the issues and giving real consideration to the adolescent's viewpoint are important. If he is unable to control his own behavior or accept direction, the earlier the limits are imposed, the better.

3. If possible, never confront an adolescent in front of his friends or in a group. At this stage of development, where peer acceptance is so important, confrontation in front of friends must be met with resistance in order to demonstrate the adolescent's dominance to peers. Confrontation should be delayed until the boys have been separated. When a group of boys are involved, they should be given as little opportunity as possible to discuss or argue issues until they can be moved into a setting where they can be separated. Boys who are involved in temporary situations will usually alter their behavior. The more hardcore, delinquent boys will maintain their resistance on an individual basis, but it will be significantly less without group support.

4. *Patience* and coolness on the part of the adult form one of the most significant approaches during confrontation with adolescents. Adolescents "looking for confrontation" must be defused. The adult should question slowly and avoid being drawn into an argument over principles or the fairness of the situation. Give the adolescent time to talk, wait for answers, allow long periods of silence, and continue to ask questions that require considered response.

5. *Never* touch or grab an adolescent during confrontation except as a means of self-defense or to prevent some physical action that will be damaging to himself or others. Touching is the most basic and significant signal of aggression, and it bypasses the use of language as a substitute for aggression. Give directions, and act as though they are expected to be obeyed. Do not threaten.

6. If necessary, give the adolescent time to "cool off" and think things over. This defusing strategy allows the adolescent to calm

13

down and reconsider his behavior. Indicate concern and, for the present, uncertainty as to a course of action. Later, approach him in a calm manner, and begin questioning without aggression.

7. As with young children, any display of kindness, such as offering food or other oral means of gratification, including cigarettes, will tend to soften many youths while they are in the cooling-off phase. Treat the problem as objectively and in as businesslike a manner as possible. Stick to the issue, and avoid moralizing during the confrontation phase. Most adolescents are well aware of what they are doing wrong, and attempts to moralize will provoke the basic issue of rebellion against what is often seen as a "messed up" adult world.

8. If arrest is not necessary, then attempt, after defusing, to get a clear, verbal commitment from the adolescent about a course of action.

9. Finally, give some assurance of belief in the boy and the expectation that he can make the right choices.

10. Recognize the adolescent's need for autonomy and right to make his own decisions. Give him the feeling that he is not being forced into choices but is being allowed to both develop and select behavior.

Further notes on aggression

Since this particular stage of adolescent development involves the adolescent's initial struggle for independence and self-identity, there is necessarily a significant component of aggression. For men in our culture, aggression is a major component of everyday behavior. Striving for autonomy and dominance forces a man to demonstrate his competence daily, and this is often illustrated in some form of aggression. Normal as it may be for the adolescent and the male adult, aggression is a very complex behavior. It should be understood that, for men, much of their very identity as men is based on some form of continuing aggression. It is not necessary to debate the appropriateness of this characteristic or to adopt the contemporary view that men should be more nurturing, sensitive, and open, as in the feminine stereotype. The concept of the nonaggressive man may be acceptable, but at present it is more a concept than a social reality. Most frequently, both male and female officers will have to deal not only with the aggression of adolescents but with their own as well, since any individual who strives to maintain a position of authority or control, as in police work, must have a strong personal orientation toward aggression. Again, there are seasoned officers who are able to work with adolescents utilizing little aggression, and this should be the goal. This is the exception rather than the rule, of course, and most officers must be prepared to use aggression and deal with it in a rational manner, both in themselves and in those whom they meet in the course of their work.

There are two major forms of aggressive behavior. The first is *overt or acting out aggression*. This is easy to recognize in adolescents and in associates. Aggression may be verbal or physical. Many men engage in aggressive verbal and physical play, such as kidding, arguing, or even shoving and pushing playfully. This is normal, and everyone has engaged in or observed such activity. The second sort of aggression is less easily recognized and is often more difficult to deal with. It is called *passive aggression*. The individual displaying passive aggression feels somewhat uncertain of himself and may have learned subtle verbal and nonverbal means of being very aggressive without the target object being certain that aggression is being displayed. For example, recent sit-ins are passive acts. They are resistive acts and therefore constitute an active form of aggression, although they are often referred to as "nonaggressive." Some individuals refuse to cooperate or talk in confrontation; this is often a passive aggressive act. Usually some distinction can be made between an adolescent who is refusing to talk out of fear or anxiety and one who is uncooperative out of hostility and passive resistance.

Aggression is a means of exerting control in a situation and is a form of "winning." Winning again leads to being dominant or controlling another person. It may simply involve winning an argument, or it may involve physical combat. Most people, including adolescent boys, hate to lose, particularly if they feel their position is the correct one. The tendency for men to desire personal control and dominance in a situation also contributes to aggression. Being accepted and wanting to join others in some mutual effort are also human needs. Although cooperation and aggression are discordant, if one can be aggressive and join with others at the same time, great feelings of exhilaration are displayed in group behavior. Unfortunately, the adolescent has not always learned socially acceptable ways of achieving this goal; this accounts for some of the dangers in officer-adolescent confrontations. Given this lack and the immaturity of the adolescent group, it is obvious that the adult must take the initiative in defusing group aggression by being as nonaggressive as the situation will allow.

THE ADOLESCENT GIRL

Girls proceed into adolescence earlier and with much more turmoil at the personal level than boys. The first and most difficult hurdle is the establishment of some sort of personal identity and role concept from models that are far more restrictive than those for boys. The glamorous roles of rock singer, movie star, and television actress are generally out of reach for most girls. The fields of computer technology, law, medicine, and various sciences that are now opening up to girls are less accessible than the media would have us believe and, in fact, do not even exist as possibilities for most of the female population. Professions such as social work, nursing, teaching, and airline stewardess are open to a larger number of girls. Highly professional roles are open and available, but their attainment requires opportunities that many girls who find themselves in confrontation with the law do not generally have.

The general culture is promoting more liberalized role models for women, but for girls from the disadvantaged group these newer roles continue to be less important than the older and more traditional roles of wife, mother, and homemaker. It is the girls from the less advantaged group who are most often incarcerated for some delinquency or crime.

Adolescent girls who are most likely to be confronted by the police officer for a serious crime are individuals from disadvantaged socioeconomic classes. This is a strong statement to make, but one merely has to visit the courts and the juvenile institutions to realize that crime is still, as it has always been, pretty much the lot of the disadvantaged. This is not to say that crime and delinquency among the advantaged class do not exist; much research suggests that crime is most prevalent in the privileged classes. However, crime in the privileged classes is often seen differently. For example, many suggest that crime among juveniles in the middle and upper socioeconomic classes is a behavior associated with temporary adjustment problems and petty in nature. The more serious crimes appear to be most prevalent in the lower and lower-middle classes.

The girls of these disadvantaged groups, although it may appear otherwise, are aspiring to be wives, mothers, and members of a secure family group. It is these girls who most concern the police officer and who deserve the majority of our concern in this discussion. The following may help to understand the young girl struggling to find some sort of personal identity and role:

1. Girls who have been successful students and recognized for various capabilities in elementary and middle school may find that acceptance into peer groups or by boys in adolescence requires that they suddenly become "dumb." "Dumb" here implies deference to boys, "cuteness," supportive behaviors toward others rather than displays of skill or achievement, and willingness to give up needs for others.

2. Attractiveness is more narrowly defined for girls than for boys. Attractiveness is very critical to the adolescent girl; however, physiological characteristics and growth rate, which are not within the girl's control, may severely limit her attractiveness in the eyes of peers.

16

3. Assertiveness or dominant and aggressive behaviors are more often punished in girls than in boys and carry more negative connotations for girls than for boys.
4. The family still places more restrictions on girls in adolescence than on boys, limiting their opportunity for personal growth and expression.
5. Adherence to classical female stereotypes provides rewards, whereas deviation tends to cause rejection and punishment. The range of acceptable behaviors for the adolescent boy, like the male stereotype, is far broader.
6. The emotional impact of the onset of menses is often far more critical for girls than the maturation process in sexual function is for boys.
7. The potential for hormonal and physiological responses that may affect behavior appears greater in the girl than in the boy.
8. Girls still tend toward "waiting game" behavior, contrary to the contemporary and popular idea that girls can be aggressive and seek out the boy. This limits the girl's ability to find positive relationships and often negates her opportunities altogether.
9. Present trends suggest that girls are returning to more conventional values concerning dating and marriage than have been generally accepted in recent years. Premarital living arrangements and various group or open relationship behaviors appear to be waning in popularity.
10. The pressures on the lower-class and lower-middle class girl are largely to grow into a woman of the classical stereotype. This limitation in role model may have an effect on the increase in violent crimes by girls during adolescence.

In the past a girl was most likely to enlarge her already accepted role of passivity and submissiveness. Today, many girls are encouraged to be more aggressive and outgoing, more assertive and dominant, and therefore the stereotype is breaking down. Families, however, generally remain more protective and restrictive with the young girl than with the boy. This is not so opposed by tradition and is mainly the result of the stability of sex-stereotyped attitudes toward women on the part of older men, such as the father.

These contrasting views of the girl's position in today's society are important to understanding her adolescent behavior. Parents of teenagers probably grew up with the typical sexual stereotypes. At the same time, the younger generation encourages girls to take a more masculine stance relative to behavior and to assert their individuality and personal rights. The girls, therefore, are often growing up in homes where parental attitudes are much the same as they have always been, while much of society

17

is encouraging them to become more assertive. This creates a greal deal of confusion for many young girls and for boys as well. There is little doubt that the more aggressive men in the culture have in fact prevented women from reaching their full potential. As women strive toward a more equal role in relationships and occupations, much turmoil is generated for both sexes. This problem has not been resolved and will continue for some years. The generation gap between what parents are still expecting of their girls and what society is attempting to foster in the way of liberation makes the situation difficult for the emerging adolescent girl. In this sense, although the behavior of boys is much the same as it always has been, the behavior of adolescent girls shows significant changes.

The male juvenile officer will be confronted with this problem, not only in the adolescent girl, but also in his fellow officers who are, in increasing numbers, women. Some girls are now adopting more assertive and dominant behaviors, while others are still playing the "waiting game." It is commonplace within some adolescent groups today for the girl to take the initiative. Girls call boys for dates, accept "Dutch" dates, and assist in determining what will be done during dates. In general, they are assuming a more equalized role in relationships. This has not been greatly discouraged by many boys who in fact enjoy this change from their father's or even older brother's day.

This changing direction in female behavior is creating many difficulties for adolescent girls in establishing their identity. There are many more options available to them, and they need not be merely passive and submissive as in the past. They need not spend so much time attempting to get boys' attention with subtle advances but can be more direct. A girl does not have to wait for the boy to decide that he likes her. She can actively pursue the boy or, as many girls do, simply ignore boys for the time being. The adolescent girl, however, is still under the early childhood influence of the home. This influence tends to condition the sensitivity, acceptance, nurturing, and emotionalism often accepted as womanly behavior. As a result, although they desire a stronger role during adolescence, girls find much conflict with parents who attempt to continue their dominance as a controlling and protective influence. Today, perhaps, there is an increase in mother-daughter conflict, since the mother is still attempting to raise her daughter as she was raised. The father may reinforce the mother, but clinical evidence indicates that as the daughter begins adolescence and appears determined to confront and challenge the mother's authority, the father is taking a more passive and confused role. The mother, unable to understand or accept her daughter's behavior, which is more aggressive and assertive than the mother desires, often develops a tremendous emotional conflict with the daughter. Thus, not only does the daughter have the traditional problem of establishing a separate identity from her mother, but she is also faced with the conflict of differing cultural values concerning appropriate behavior for girls.

In such a situation, the father, although remaining somewhat passive, tends to take such an arbitrary and immovable stance that he becomes totally ineffective in relating to his daughter. "After all, this is just a girl." Of course, in many homes the father maintains the traditional role of expecting the girl to be passive, while the mother subtly encourages the daughter's newly found independence, which she herself secretly desires. The girl also has the tremendous social pressure placed on women in the culture that demands, on one hand, "Be more independent than your mother was," and, on the other, "Remember, good girls act like girls."

In addition, the girl has all of the traditional difficulties associated with her changing physiological structure, the onset of menstruation, and general physical growth. Biologically, she has a strong drive toward femininity, but a social counterdrive exists toward establishment of a new independence for all women. All of this has the effect of causing more conflict and turmoil for adolescent girls than for boys. The girl is often confused, angry, and frustrated in her attempts to decide who she is, what she believes, and how she will behave.

Relative to many family, school, and personal factors, girls enter adolescence with tremendous anxiety. Depending on the various factors operating, many girls do quite well, whereas others do very poorly. It may be safe to say that girls have a greater potential for divergence in behavior than do boys. The major goal for both girls and boys is to establish a beachhead of independence and personal identity.

Some general guidelines concerning initial approach to girls follow:

1. Do not patronize girls or use typical male attitudes toward women. Treat them as individuals, and respect their attitudes and feelings, as a man might with a boy. Don't expect certain traditional behaviors of girls simply because they are girls.

2. All of the defusing behaviors used with boys also apply to girls. In fact, they may be more important since girls tend to be more resistant and negative in an attempt to overcompensate for what they feel will be patronizing and chauvinistic attitudes from men.

3. As with boys, never touch or grab adolescent girls, except as a means of defense or to protect them from self-abuse and destructive behaviors.

4. Don't be put down or turned off because girls use abusive or profane language. Such language should be treated in the same manner as when used by a boy, with no less attention and certainly no

more. As with boys, such language is simply a verbal means of expressing hostility and is preferable to physical acting out.

5. Men are often conditioned to place little value in the logic or sensibility of what women say. However, women are as logical and intelligent as men and, in some ways, much more so. Thus, place just as much value on what the adolescent girl says as on what is said by a boy in confrontation. Listen to her, and discuss the logic and appropriateness of what is being said rather than who is saying it.

6. Attempt to avoid aggressive nonverbal behavior or behavior that implies dominance. Give the girl room to move, and assume that she will comply with the adult's expectations.

7. Immediately eliminate feelings that girls are overly emotional and that their behavior is due to typical female emotionalism. Apparent emotionalism in women may well be a more honest expression of feelings than is encountered in men. Thus, when confronting an adolescent girl or group of girls, do not overreact to their general behavior. Stay calm, observe their behavior, and listen to what they are saying rather than how they are saying it.

8. As with boys, give the girls time to think. Do not become overly punitive and expect immediate compliance. Usually, when girls are treated with some dignity and as if they are responsible, they respond more quickly than boys by talking things over in a frank manner.

9. All of the guidelines for approaching boys also apply to girls, including avoidance of a confrontation with an individual in front of the group. Peer group belonging is as strong for the girl as it is for the boy.

SUMMARY

With the understanding that boys and girls are different and that the culture will probably continue to so socialize them in different ways, we offer the following concepts of treatment regardless of the sex of the individual. Adolescents should be:

1. Recognized as individuals and given the same respect, consideration, and acceptance regardless of sex.
2. Given an opportunity to demonstrate their individuality.
3. Encouraged to make decisions themselves without the assumption that their sex role precludes decision-making skills.
4. Treated as objectively as possible in confrontation regardless of sex.
5. Given the opportunity to learn new skills or develop more independence in job-related learning in accordance with their personal desires and motivation regardless of sex.

6. Encouraged to set personal and occupational goals toward which they feel motivated, regardless of sexual differences.
7. Encouraged to develop definite personal values and attitudes regardless of sex role expectations.
8. Expected to adhere to social rules and alter behavior toward successful community adjustment.

Both boys and girls go through an initial stage of development on entering adolescence. During this stage physiological changes create not only new physical form but new feelings. Both boys and girls enter a stage where personal identity is the goal, and this is most often expressed through identity with a group. Girls will tend to display more frustration and confusion on entering adolescence than will boys because of the conflict between contemporary attitudes toward feminine behavior and more traditional views.

There are many indications that an important variable in becoming liberated, for boys and girls, is socioeconomic advantage. The lower-class boy must depend more on strength, cunning, street wisdom, and the use of aggression to improve his status and group membership for security than his more advantaged upper-middle and upper-class counterpart. The lower-class girl must also depend more on her sexuality, her role as a supporter of a dominant male for security, and her nurturing capacity than her counterpart in the upper-middle and upper-class culture. Equality of the sexes is not only a very sophisticated cultural concept, it requires occupational opportunity, knowledge, family encouragement and acceptance, and special social skills and expertise. An important and integral aspect of these conditions is language development and competence. Educability and language growth provide the opportunity for the individual to learn, to thoughtfully evaluate choices, and to increase his own awareness of those around him.

When one views the population of adolescents most likely to come into conflict with the law, it becomes apparent that the lower and lower-middle socioeconomic groups most often find themselves in some sort of confrontation. It is also at this level of cultural status that the sexual stereotypes are most frequently reinforced. Thus, adolescent growth for these girls is most likely to occur in relationship to stereotyped behaviors.

For the boy, emergence into adolescence is accompanied by many of the male cultural traditions of dominance, independence, aggression, assertion, and status. As we discussed earlier in the chapter, although personal identity and role are the foundations of behavioral growth, the role of the boy includes the classical male orientation. The girl also struggles with personal identity and role, but often this role is manifested in the traditional female stereotypes: nurturing, passive, dependent, and other culturally defined characteristics of women. The emphasis in today's media on women's liberation and the Equal Rights Amendment suggests that there is a great movement throughout the country toward equalization of the male-female occupational and familial roles. However, when one looks at the middle to lower socioeconomic groups, one discovers much less enthusiasm for the women's movement. Instead, one often finds that, for much of the population, there has been little change in recent years in the actual roles to which boys and girls are socialized. Even in upper-middle and upper-class adolescents, there is an increasing tendency today to return to more traditional role expectations.

ADDITIONAL READINGS

Adams, J. *Understanding adolescence: Current developments in adolescent psychology.* Boston: Allyn & Bacon, 1976.

Kiell, N. *The universal experience of adolescence.* Boston: International Universities Press and Beacon Press, 1964.

McCandless, B. R. *Adolescents: Behavior and development.* Hinsdale, Ill.: Dryden Press, 1970.

Ruch, F. *Psychology and life.* Glenview, Ill.: Scott Foresman, 1967.

CHAPTER 2

CLASSIFICATIONS OF BEHAVIOR

I had no decision in my birth,
But I will have to decide on my life.

In the first chapter, we discussed some general aspects of adolescent behavior. The major crisis in adolescence is that of establishing an identity that is distinct from the family. This natural tendency is of emerging not only as a person but as one who has a feeling of "wholeness" and unity within. The child is protected by family, school values, and authority during elementary school; therefore, identity is maintained within the framework of school and home characteristics. This framework provides security and identity for the child. He understands who he is because he understands his role and position, and he is reassured by the knowledge. The elementary school years are, consequently, continuous, and the child proceeds with a frame of personal reference that is more or less stable.

DISCONTINUITY OF ADOLESCENCE

During adolescence, because of the need to alter past patterns of behavior and identity, the individual is suddenly thrust into a role that has no family or school integration. The adolescent finds himself unable to accept his past role or, in many cases, unwilling to agree to the values and expectations that adults have for him. For a period of time, as the adolescent struggles to develop some sort of independent self-identity, he feels lost, confused, and often uncertain of where he is going or who he is, but certain that he needs to make some sort of change. This period can be called a time of personal discontinuity. The adolescent feels cut off from the past and without any new framework of orientation in the present or future. His life has been disrupted, and daily activities that were routine in the past now become boring or unacceptable. During this time, the adolescent searches for information from peers, and such activity often lays the basis for the strong drive toward peer group belonging.

This period of discontinuity may last for a few months, or it might even extend into adulthood. Where the adolescent has developed strong interests at school or in the community that give him recognition and status, the period of discontinuity may pass without notice or may not even occur. Many adolescents find the period of initial identity search frustrating and even frightening. During this period several possibilities exist that may lead the adolescent into conflict with the laws of the community. In this chapter, several syndromes of behavioral difficulties will be briefly reviewed to assist the juvenile officer in understanding the basis for certain disruptive behaviors in juveniles.

BEHAVIORAL CLASSIFICATION OF DEVIANCE IN THE ADOLESCENT

The classification of behavior generally comprises a number of characteristics: physical, socioeconomic, race and religious affiliation, general attitudes, education, and several other descriptors. Frequently the juvenile officer is less familiar with psychological or behavioral classification. There are many terms used to describe various conditions that indicate abnormal psychological growth. To confuse the issue, many of the terms used in psychological literature and in sociology are defined differently in varying situations and when used by a variety of professionals in the mental health field.

The following classifications are examples of some typical ways in which adolescent behavior can be described. We have found these to be particularly useful in regard to adolescents described as delinquent.

Adolescent adjustment reaction

There are major phases of life change for us all. The first phase of our life is infancy, which begins at birth and ends at 18 months to 2 years. The beginning of the next phase, early childhood, is marked by increased awareness, use of language, exploratory behaviors, and the development of a personal concept. This phase ends usually at about 5 or 6 years of age, when the child begins formal schooling. The latter period is marked by increased independence, physical separation from the home, and the beginning of childhood, which will continue until adolescence. Adolescence begins roughly at the age of 13 and continues through the teen years, ending at about 19, the beginning of young adulthood. Other life phases follow throughout our lifetime, and each one is marked by physiological, psychological, sociological, and intellectual changes that require adjustment in the individual's life style and personal concept. Adolescent adjustment is perhaps one of the most critical because the changes are so marked. Adolescents respond to this crisis of change in a variety of ways. Some adolescents, unable to face the reality of their emerging independence and personal growth, have severe emotional reactions. This sort of difficulty is often indicated by adults with phrases such as, "He is acting like an adolescent," or "He is going through one of his phases." Adolescents remark that, "He hasn't got it together," or "He's spacey." Phrases change with time, but each generation has its own collection of terms and idiomatic descriptions that denote a difference in behavior between one individual and others. The *adolescent adjustment reaction* is the professional correlate to the popular terms used by parents and adolescent peers to indicate these deviations in behavior. Mental health professionals may use the term to describe an adolescent who is exhibiting some form of behavioral deviance but who, on examination, does not exhibit long-term and significant personality or social dysfunction that would imply a more dramatic disorder.

Adolescents who display temporary but dramatic changes in behavior and adjustment may be individuals who, for a variety of personal and sociological reasons, are unable to adjust to the changes that affect a person during adolescence. These individuals may become negative, aggressive, and hostile, or they may assume a posture of depression, withdrawal, and drug involvement and even have temporary episodes of suicidal tendencies, all of which eventually give way to more normalized behaviors. This is why parent counseling, adolescent group therapy programs, and various school and community assistance programs for adolescents and families who need help are so important. With proper understanding and assistance, adolescents who display problematic adjustment reactions can usually proceed through the temporary crisis toward eventual adjustment.

There are many causes for the development of an adolescent adjustment reaction. The adolescent may be an individual who has been very sheltered during his life, and the increasing demand for independence and the approach of the time for finally leaving the family circle may cause extreme anxiety and depression. The depressive behavior may stimulate anxiety in the parents and overconcern about the adolescent's withdrawal and unwillingness to talk about his "problem." This reaction, in turn, may reinforce the adolescent's alarm and stimulate further depression. Other adolescents may be quite capable and independent before adolescence and, as they enter this phase, may demand more opportunity to make their own decisions before parents are willing to grant such freedom. Continued resistance and negativism between such adolescents and parents can result in an increasing hostility in the adolescent that eventuates in overt and delinquent acts. The key to the adolescent adjustment reaction is the recognition that it has its roots in personal and family characteristics that often have to be sorted out by someone outside the situation, who can objectively outline and illustrate the dynamics of the situation. This often requires mental health intervention.

The rebel

The rebel syndrome in the adolescent boy. The "rebel" is an adolescent faced with two problems. He must establish an identity separate from his parents, and this identity must be one that will gain peer acceptance. If the boy has not been too successful in school or if the home is authoritarian, requiring additional force to gain freedom, then he may have to overcompensate in order to "make his break." Consequently, the rebel becomes more resistive and negative toward authority than he has been in the past. His rebellion is not so much calculated rebellion as merely an unconscious statement that he wishes to "be different," that he wants and needs autonomy and independence. He attacks all authority through personal criticism, resistance, and belligerence. If the parent, teacher, or juvenile officer takes a punitive or authoritarian approach toward the boy, his resistance increases, and he may be driven further from any possible help from adults. He may be quite argumentative, simply for the sake of resisting any control over his behavior.

The rebel requires moderate limits and a great deal of positive encouragement to talk out his feelings. Aggression toward him should be kept at a minimum, with the adult supporting his independence and, at the same time, constantly encouraging him to engage in whatever situation he finds himself. The rebel requires an adult-adolescent contact to set expectations for his behavior. This satisfies his need to maintain independence and develop it into a personal feeling of control. In most cases the rebel is a boy who, as he establishes identity and personal responsibility, will become more cooperative, similar to the individual he was before the disruption caused by the temporary discontinuity.

One of the most common errors of parents is their confusion and panic when their son or daughter suddenly becomes negative, when in the past they have been "normal" or even "ideal" children. This panic often takes the form of stronger limits or even rejection of the adolescent, which in turn increases the adolescent's hostility and confusion. Often, patience and positive support will accomplish more than will increased limits and control by authority figures.

During this period of rebellion, the adolescent is very vulnerable to many external influences that can complicate or even increase hostility and discontinuity. If, during this period of negativeness, the adolescent happens to initiate associations with delinquent youths, he may adopt their personal identity. This association will not only prolong his rebellion but may increase it until he becomes a chronic behavior problem. Conversely, if the adolescent manintains his healthy associations with peers from the community, then the members of the peer group may eventually aid each other sympathetically toward more positive behaviors. This frequently occurs, but the adolescent who is accepted into a truly deviant or delinquent group creates the most concern for parents and juvenile officers. This possibility requires that parents attempt to watch peer group selection by their adolescent during this period. Negative experiences with teachers or juvenile law officers could also tend to push the rebel into more extreme and long-lasting behavioral deviancy. The adults' approach to such problems is crucial to the outcome.

The rebel syndrome in the adolescent girl. The adolescent girl today has come under increased attention because of the many girls who are displaying delinquent behavior. In the past, girls were most often found to be accessories to crimes committed by boys. The well-known prototype of this girl is "hard," "promiscuous," and "easily led." The image still exists for much of the population, but today additional forms of female delinquency have emerged. The adolescent girl today may exhibit many of the same syndromes as boys, although some differences do exist.

During the campus disorders in the late 1960's and early 1970's, many women emerged as participants and leaders in group actions, with unifying causes including student rights, women's rights, and political ideologies. These women, although often part of a group led primarily by men, demonstrated much individualism and a special aggressiveness formerly expected only of men. The adolescent girl who has been reared in an environment of liberalism may attempt to establish both her personal identity and a role in the current struggle for women's rights. The individuals who attempt to establish their identity in radical groups are often women who are honestly attempting to become more total individuals than their mothers have been. However, because of the nature of the groups or the situation in which they find themselves, their activity may extend beyond the usual adolescent rebellion and become decidedly criminal and dangerous.

The radical leaders in the women's groups who went beyond sensible and acceptable rebellion have, interestingly enough, somewhat cooled on reaching their early thirties. This suggests that the tendency is for these individuals to finally establish a more or less stable adult identity. Although they would hate to admit it, much of the ferment for which they were responsible was a combination of real social change and, unfortunately, a passing phase like that experienced by all adolescents. The time and political mood of the country simply provided a more dramatic stage than is usually available to the rebellious adolescent.

In addition to the temporary rebellion of the radical fighting for rights and political change, there have been many other effects that have not been as easily sold to the media. There are many girls today who, like their sisters in the late 1960's, feel a personal need for more self-expression, freedom, and equality in the community. Unfortunately, many of these girls are loners who look toward the role models with fewer capabilities than are needed to perpetrate a recognizable and significant rebellion. These girls are left with fewer ways of attempting to establish themselves. The most frequent routes for these girls to take are ones that lead away from the oppressive, in their view, atmosphere of home and school. In recent years, more and more girls from all walks of life have taken to the streets, highways, or roads in search of something they do not clearly understand. Most of these girls are not running to something but away from what they consider to be an unjust and unloving world at home. Strangely, many of these girls are neither girls with deep psychological problems nor girls who are typically delinquent. They are girls searching for their time, a place for themselves that is somehow different from what they have seen in their families. There is little doubt that the women's movement, the changing roles of women in general, and the need to become both a woman and a person have all combined to foster the increase in runaway girls. But their basic motivation appears to be a rebellion against what they consider an inappropriate and unnecessary life style.

Rebellious girls unfortunately find much less status in their rebellion in that, because of continuing stereotypes for men and women, their male contemporaries end up leading them in their runaway syndrome. For the girls who run away to escape a male chauvinist world that oppresses them as women, the confrontation with the total society, including their runaway friends, is not only less than they had hoped but worse than they had imagined. While Helen Reddy or some other women's rights model sings away on the radio of how to be a person and a woman, the runaway girl often finds herself in some dingy apartment or "collective" still washing dishes and waiting on the men just as her mother did.

The rebellious girl may engage in a variety of delinquent acts, as do boys, or may eventually join a religious cult that promises, although little individualism, an identity that transcends that of sex. In the adolescent group, the religious cult, or the group living arrangement, the girl begins to find what she is seeking: an identity of some kind that she can use to mold her own self-concept.

The rebellious girl, like her male counterpart, needs understanding, acceptance, and time. Most of the girls who are actively seeking some sort of identity will eventually tend toward some form of adult authority and acceptance. Counseling and mental health intervention can often bring these girls into a mode of successful growth. The girls who do end up in courts can be particularly trying, for they are often fiercely determined to assert themselves and to establish a personal identity that is not dependent on the typical female role in society. This resistance can eventually take them headlong into confrontation with law enforcement agencies and may be so great that they must be institutionalized for a period of time until they can be assisted through their dilemma.

Neurotic reactions

Neurosis is a clinical term that designates an emotional reaction to the environment by an individual. This syndrome is usually characterized by various fears, anxiety, physical and emotional reactions to stress, and a variety of maladaptive behaviors. The nature of neurotic behavior is complex, but a keynote in recognizing such difficulties is that the individual usually retains functional ability. In psychotic and schizoid reactions, there is usually a strong element of thought disorder; however, the neurotic individual is able to continue to function intellectually. The neurotic individual, then, often has many emotionally based difficulties

29

but is usually able to maintain contact with the reality of his world, in contrast to the psychotic individual.

Neurotic behavior is usually found in childhood and emotional development and is often a problem that is somewhat long-standing. As opposed to the adolescent undergoing a temporary and dramatic adjustment reaction, the neurotic adolescent often displays a history of poor adaptive behavior. The neurotic adolescent may be unable to maintain emotional stability and often looks to his environment to explain away his unusual fears and anxiety. Often he is an individual who has long-term feelings of failure, helplessness, incompetence, and unworthiness. Sometimes these feelings are manifested in or blamed on various physical difficulties, such as headaches, fatigue, poor physical stature, and unattractiveness; ineptness in sports or school; poor mental abilities; or general lack of opportunity. The neurotic individual develops many ways of dealing with his anxiety or emotional difficulties. He may overcompensate for feelings of inadequacy through aggressive acts, through "tough guy" roles, or by assuming a posture of negativism toward others. Some neurotic persons take the route of attempting to "talk" their way to acceptance by others. They may brag about their conquests, overstate their past achievements, and attempt to "fool" others into believing they are highly successful individuals. Others become alcoholics, drug users, or hypochondriacs in an attempt to escape their own feelings of hopelessness and fear. Thus it is not surprising that many neurotic adolescents choose criminal activity in an effort to achieve some measure of success quickly without the necessity of a time-consuming struggle to develop real skills. The neurotic delinquent may feel that criminal acts punish others for the wrongs suffered during his lifetime. Perverse and daring crimes may give the neurotic individual a sense of importance, status, or power that, for a time, alleviates his feelings of failure.

Neurotic reactions are very common and are neither easily identified nor changed. Some examples of this type of behavior follow.

The delinquent neurotic syndrome in the adolescent boy. The rebel is often a boy who temporarily displays deviant and negative behaviors because of an identity crisis in adolescence. Most often, the crisis passes, and independence is established. However, as juvenile officers know, there are also aggressive and rebellious boys who have displayed this behavioral pattern in elementary years. *Neurotic* generally implies that an individual has feelings of anxiety, fear, and hostility that stem from personality difficulties rather than from a transitory adjustment problem. Frequently, the neurotic child has been mistreated at home, has been a chronic school failure, or has not developed a healthy self-image during childhood and has subsequently been unable to do so.

The delinquent neurotic child needs mental health intervention.

30

Waiting for the storm to pass or giving the neurotic adolescent more time to work through his identity crisis usually will not be effective. The neurotic boy often associates with other boys who are chronic truants and incorrigible individuals. Unfortunately, the school and community agencies available to parents have not been very successful in assisting these children. If such intervention is effective, the child is obviously not a continual problem. But when an adolescent with a long history of behavioral deviancy is encountered by the juvenile officer, it is probable that the school and community have failed to successfully intervene. Then the responsibility falls to the law enforcement officer.

Experience shows that, in general, the entire legal system, from law enforcement agencies to the courts, tends to be overly liberal with these adolescents. Adults involved with an adolescent would like to help him, particularly when it is obvious that emotional and family problems exist. However, such boys often find themselves in court for repeated offenses before any real intervention is initiated. The earlier some form of intervention occurs, the more likely it is to be successful. Undoubtedly, this will remain a problem because of varying views held by community agencies and law officials concerning the appropriateness and effectiveness of correctional treatment. These boys need strong limits and controls and specialized treatment. Unfortunately, such assistance is often possible only in institutional settings or group homes. Whatever resources are available should be used, and they should be used much earlier than is customary. If the juvenile officer can judge whether a boy's behavior results from a temporary adjustment reaction or from an actual neurotic reaction, juvenile treatment will be more effective. However, it will remain the job of the juvenile officer to make this decision in the field. Decision making of this kind requires much training and professional growth on the part of the juvenile officer. It would be more appropriate if adequate diagnostic services and treatment programs existed in which such decisions could be made. Realistically, the juvenile officer will probably remain not only a law enforcer, but also a social worker, probation counselor, and judge. He needs to be prepared as adequately as possible for this role; however, too often the higher levels of training are reserved for individuals in jobs where such training is least effective. If many of the court and probation personnel had to serve an annual period of time in the field confronting adolescents, they would probably drastically alter many of their ideas about treatment.

The neurotic delinquent is a boy who has personality disorders that create anxiety, uncertainty, and fear in his relationships with adults and authority figures. He is often a boy who enters the adolescent period with a high degree of already existent discontinuity that is intensified by the role expectations of peers and adults and by his own drastically changing

31

physiological system. For these reasons, the neurotic boy needs mental health intervention, and it is important for the juvenile officer to spend some time investigating the youth's general school and family history. Enforcement of the law with such a boy is important as a means of providing him security and protection from his own anxiety, but the ultimate goal should be to provide him with the necessary help for his personal and familial mental health. The neurotic delinquent often over-reacts to confrontation with police officers. His problems revolve around personal uncertainty, confusion, anxiety, and fear, causing him to become panic-striken when he is actually confronted by authority. This panic may take the form of blind rage or aggression, or flight and escape. If the boy's reaction takes an aggressive form, he should be subdued as soon as possible and taken to a safe and secure place to calm down and collect his thoughts. He should be handled with as little aggression as possible because his panic could lead him to irrational and dangerous acts that he would be temporarily unable to control. This aggressive reaction is one of blind, raging fear and not calculated or directed anger. This is important since it is entirely different from the reaction of a boy showing actual anger and hostility. Physical restraints and continuous reassurance will often calm the neurotic boy until he is able to collect himself, realize that he will not be hurt, and that there is no need for alarm.

If the boy attempts to run or withdraw, then all measures should be taken to comfort and reassure him and to provide a situation in which he feels safe. It is extremely important to realize that the neurotic boy who expresses his fear by running is not only in need of reassurance but potentially suicidal. When extremely fearful or in a threatened position, some individuals may become self-destructive in order to escape. This is an irrational reaction, but in a state of panic the boy will not be able to reason out or evaluate his situation on his own. In both the aggressive and flight-prone neurotic boy, reassurance, protection, and containment are of utmost importance until he has regained some control of himself.

The neurotic syndrome in the adolescent girl. Girls are no less prone to neurotic behavior than boys, although some professionals would like to argue this point. One of the major problems for the adolescent girl has traditionally been some form of neurotic behavior. Her emerging identity as a woman, although it may include individualism, often is directed toward a nurturing and loving relationship. A significant number of teenage girls enter relationships and groups in order to find someone to love and to be loved by to compensate for a lack of love and attention at home. The case of an adolescent girl who is drawn into a supposed "loving" relationship and then left high, dry, and pregnant is an old story. The girl, seeking to compensate for the absence of love in the home, may even desire a baby in order to have someone who will love her. This is also a traditional syndrome. The increased availability of contraceptives has made it possible for girls to take a more aggressive role with boys without the fear of unwanted pregnancy, but the freedom gained from birth control pills, for the neurotic girl seeking love and affection, often becomes the hell that they wished to escape. The boy, often more copulation-oriented than loving, finds the liberated girl the girl of his adolescent dreams, someone he can enjoy in bed without fear and leave without regret. Such relationships are often more sexually oriented than loving, and the neurotic girl may be plunged into relationship after relationship in an attempt to gain what little love she can from these transitory sexual encounters. She often still finds herself taken advantage of as she felt she was in her love-deprived family. The situation can plunge her into more severe neurotic behavior, such as prostitution and delinquency, with accompanying rejection of real feeling or emotion.

These girls, as do neurotic boys, need mental health intervention. The increased number of women in law enforcement has made available many new special personnel to meet the needs of these girls, including problems associated with pregnancy and rape. Certainly law enforcement agencies must recognize that men may not have the necessary knowledge or empathy to understand these girls, whether in the streets, courts, or institutions. Unfortunately, many aspects of the legal system today do not recognize the importance of the development of more specialized services to help the delinquent girl. However, time appears to be on the side of the girls, and changes are being made.

Psychotic and schizoid reactions

Psychosis is a term used clinically to designate a wide range of personality disorders, usually associated with mental disorientation and dysfunction. "Mental" is used here to designate intellectual function as opposed to the emotional difficulties of the neurotic individual. The neurotic person who demonstrates feelings of incompetence certainly has a variety of intellectual, or "mental," difficulties. However, in the case of the psychotic person, although many emotional components are present, the primary difficulty exists in perception, objectivity, and distinguishing reality from the unreal. Although the neurotic individual is generally capable of recognizing the reality of his behavior and that of others, he is not willing to accept it, nor can he deal with his emotional reactions to the environment. The psychotic person may be unable to distinguish the unreal aspects that he attributes to the environment from what is really there. In some individuals, psychotic behavior is totally pervasive, and they must be institutionalized or placed in long-term therapy. However, there are many individuals who have lesser degrees of psychosis and individuals who display certain forms of psychotic behavior that do not preclude their minimal adjustment to the community. The severely psychotic person has difficulty in even minimal adjustment to an independent life style, but some forms of psychotic behavior are more subtle and may go undetected for some time. Psychosis, like neurosis, is usually based on long-standing and rather dramatic conditions, although some forms of temporary psychosis may be related to episodes of neurological and biophysical dysfunction. Much of the current research on psychotic behavior supports a stronger biological basis for an increasing number of psychotic classifications.

Psychotic behavior in adolescents can take many forms and usually is cause for considerable alarm. One of the classical forms of psychotic behavior that the police officer may encounter is that of the paranoid personality. The individual is unable to clearly and objectively relate his own behavior to consequences and believes that others intend him harm. Such an individual is capable of horrendous crimes or bizarre behavior that to him appears perfectly logical. Here we find the pathological behaviors that result in murder with no understandable basis. Individuals who have committed mass murders, stationed themselves on top of buildings and shot several people, mutilated the bodies of murder victims, or committed sex-related murders have often been psychotic persons.

The psychotic individual whose condition is based on either personality disorders or an organic problem requires treatment from mental health professionals. The police officer will find attempts to involve the psychotic individual in some sort of rational interaction a difficult, if not impossible, task. However, there are conditions under which an individual may temporarily enter a psychotic state, and there are people who live their lives in a prepsychotic state. In these cases, the individual may appear relatively normal at times and be able to perform basic independent acts without appearing different from those around him. However, a number of conditions and situations may stimulate an escape into a psychotic episode. A lack of rational behavior and a tendency to engage in fantasy to the exclusion of reality are important signs for the police officer. In addition to paranoid syndromes, there are other forms of psychotic behavior, including manic and depressive states, hallucinations, feelings of grandeur, unfounded feelings of persecution, and a wide range of irrational beliefs and ideas. Another form of severe personality and intellectual difficulty is found in the schizoid personality. Although this individual may exhibit a variety of personality symptoms as does the psychotic person, the schizoid person often manifests a separation of intellectual and emotional life. These individuals may repress or, for

34

some reason, have never developed a normal emotional basis for their behavior. They intellectualize and rationalize the world, devoid of feeling and emotion.

The sociopathic person is an individual who appears to operate without a consistent value structure and who is often seemingly devoid of normal feelings of guilt that most individuals exhibit. The sociopathic individual is very difficult to deal with because he tends to be an opportunist without anxiety over his behavior. The sociopathic person can commit various criminal acts and find no emotional reason to alter his behavior. The means justify the end for this individual; he will lie to, deceive, and manipulate those around him to gain his ends.

The sociopathic syndrome in the adolescent boy. Some boys confront the adolescent period of discontinuity in a unique way that should alert the juvenile officer with all the force of horns blowing, bombs going off, or a major assault from an enemy attack force. This adjustment reaction to discontinuity is the *sociopathic syndrome.* The sociopathic boy neither adheres to nor accepts the traditional value structure of the society. He operates from a totally different base of personal belief than do other, even neurotic, adolescents. The boy with a sociopathic reaction has either learned or developed what to him is a rational way of viewing himself and the world. The rule of behavior is the belief that whatever works is right since the world is filled with double standards and fakes. This reaction is usually based in family and cultural differences. The youth may adhere, at least loosely, to the general value structure of the school until he is thrust into the difficulties associated with adolescence. While he is young and somewhat powerless, he may adhere to school expectations and even home authority; thus, he has not previously been viewed as a severe problem requiring special attention.

The sociopathic adolescent often displays many of the general tendencies of social pathology very early in his school experience. He tends to take advantage of situations in order to avoid responsibility or adherence to the rules set for most children. He finds little value in concentrating on achievement as an acceptable goal, and his work often reflects a lack of concern, if not blatant resistance, to teacher demands. Often the sociopathic boy will try to defer facing problems or project the blame for his own behavior on parents, teachers, or peers. He may have a history of truancy and minor infractions of school regulations. Relationships with other children are those in which he controls others or rejects them if they do not accept his leadership. There is often a lack of appropriate emotional response to attention from adults or other children. He may even seem to be very objective and intelligent, and adults may see this as the reason that he has difficulty relating. As he gains status and success in the deviant culture, he finally resolves his discontinuity by accepting a personal belief system that is opposed to the law, society, and any organized and traditional social structure.

The normal adolescent who finds himself in temporary conflict with authority can usually be encouraged toward normal behaviors, since he continues to maintain typical social and personal values although he is temporarily testing the effectiveness of those values and attitudes. In contrast, the sociopathic individual is operating on deviant values and beliefs. Thus, the juvenile officer will be confronted with an adolescent who, unlike the normal adolescent, will not feel guilt or remorse for his deviant acts. The absence of guilt is significant, for the emergence of feelings of guilt is a major factor in the normal adolescent's positive change in behavior. The sociopathic adolescent is capable of using almost any means to accomplish his ends, including physical violence and extreme measures of resistance or force. The sociopathic adolescent responds to legal confrontation with a hardened determination to resist, to fight, and to eventually win in the game against society and authority. He may use threats or even physical violence in reaction to authority. If that doesn't work or is not to his advantage, he may be submissive and appear to comply with authority. However, as soon as the threat is removed, he will return to his original behavior pattern.

The sociopathic syndrome in the adolescent girl. It is interesting that most mental health professionals and law enforcement officers generally think of a boy as sociopathic rather than a girl. Girls do become sociopathic. However, here the police officer may develop an insight into the weakness of mental health terminology. "Sociopathic behavior" appears rather well defined as it is used to describe certain kinds of male behavior. However, the description does not seem to fit the adolescent girl as well. If we refer back to the sociopathic boy, we see that the major characteristic is an absence of guilt over his behavior. He tends to be an opportunist who feels the means justify the end. He is manipulative and often clever in his verbal handling of confrontation. These characteristics are also found in girls. A girl can display sociopathic behavior; however, stereotyped family attitudes toward girls often preclude the emergence of social pathology as early in the girl as in the boy. Boys are taught to be aggressive and competitive and are expected to take a dominant and assertive role. This conditioning can bring the boy into a sociopathic role more easily than the girl, who is taught to be subservient, nurturing, submissive, and *guilty.*

Thus, if all things were equal, a boy under certain conditions might become sociopathic, whereas a girl would become neurotic, persistent in her aggressive and hostile behavior. Perhaps girls who do demonstrate social pathology are more often girls raised in homes where the conventional attitudes toward girls are not present. It would be difficult to demonstrate this probability, but it is offered here for the police officer's consideration.

How should the sociopathic girl be treated? Girls who are sociopathic must be treated in much the same manner as boys. The sociopathic girl will be manipulative, perhaps even attempting to seduce the male officer, and will show little or no apparent guilt or concern over her behavior. These girls require definite limits and extended assistance by mental health personnel. However, as in the case of sociopathic boys, mental health professionals have not been highly successful in changing the basic personality of the sociopathic girl.

Although in reading the following section it may seem that little difference exists between the sociopathic and the primitive and unsocialized individual, there are differences, and they will affect the ways in which the two individuals should be confronted. First, the primitive and unsocialized individual, although often appearing to operate without values, in fact frequently has a very strong sense of guilt and trust. The sociopathic individual demonstrates an absence of guilt about his behavior. The primitive and unsocialized person, chaotic as his relationships may be, seeks out relationships and often attempts to maintain them under the most adverse conditions; the sociopathic individual appears unable to form responsible relationships. The primitive and unsocialized individual may not even know that a law exists, but the sociopathic person knows what the law is and what its weaknesses may be. The primitive and unsocialized individual breaks the law by default or anger and frustration; the sociopathic individual breaks it for his advantage and because he sees it as stupid and constricting.

Primitive and unsocialized behavior

Many individuals come into contact with the law because they have been unable or have not had the opportunity to become responsible citizens. These individuals range from those who are only marginally intelligent to those who have been culturally deprived and have not had the necessary education and opportunity to learn how to effectively deal with the larger community in which they live.

Some mental health professionals use the term *primitive and unsocialized* to describe individuals who display an actual personality disorder as opposed to individuals who exhibit poor adjustment as a consequence of low mentality or a lack of social opportunity and learning or come from cultural subgroups that are economically and socially depressed. However, there have been cases in which individuals had been so mistreated in childhood that they were not only poorly adjusted but not socialized at all. These are the rare instances in which a child has been locked up in an attic or basement since early childhood. However, this

37

designation generally refers to individuals who have poor educational, economic, emotional, and social environments but make a marginal adjustment to society.

At this point in the discussion, we need to discount the myth that primitive and unsocialized individuals are always the product of economic or cultural deprivation. This is not the case, although such an individual is most often a person who has come from a deprived environment. Certainly, primitive and unsocialized behaviors do not result simply from being poor. The primitive and unsocialized individual comes from a family that is often deprived; but, more important, he has parents who meet none of the requirements for effectively rearing children. This second factor lays the basis for primitive and, frequently, impulsive acting out behavior. The adolescent boy or girl from such an environment requires not only an effective learning environment but also mental health treatment.

The primitive and unsocialized syndrome in the adolescent boy. It is unlikely that an adolescent would like to be labeled "primitive and unsocialized," but the term is very descriptive of the reaction syndrome to discontinuity. Often boys with low mentality and educational skills will react to adolescence with confusion and negativeness. Primitive and unsocialized boys are not always limited in mental capacity, however; many boys who have had difficulty learning, who have been on the fringe of social interaction, or who simply have never learned effective social behaviors will also exhibit this behavioral syndrome. There is a little primitive tendency in everyone. If one likes something, he wants it. It may be a member of the opposite sex, power, status, or money. But most people control themselves and seek socially acceptable ways of satisfying needs. The adolescent who functions on the primitive level, however, is unable to control his own pleasure-seeking instinct. In this respect, he might be compared with an infant. An infant is not concerned with socially accepted ways of meeting his needs. He wants only to be comfortable and well fed. He will display any behavior, appropriate or not, in order that those needs be met. Similarly, the adolescent who is interested only in his immediate needs will behave in whatever way is necessary to meet those needs.

The primitive and unsocialized individual is difficult to deal with because of a lack of personal and social responsibility and an almost driven tendency toward hedonistic activity. These boys are pleasure seekers, not law breakers, but their clumsy and uninhibited behavior often results in confrontation with teachers, police officers, and the community at large. Many such individuals in small communities or in particularly close-knit cultural groups are tolerated by others, although their status in the community is usually very low. They may work part-time at unskilled jobs and use their earnings to buy things, pleasure, and high-status cars. Here the gaudy, overpowered, supercar syndrome of adolescence is most apparent.

For the primitive and unsocialized individual, immediate gratification and continuous pleasure-seeking behavior are the goals of life. Attending school or working is only an interlude, a way to obtain money, or an opportunity to exhibit oneself or find some new way to feel a thrill. Usually these adolescents do not want to break the law. Their real goal is simply to have fun and "get it on" as often as possible. It is incidental to them that the law sometimes gets in the way. To this group confrontation is a dangerous thing. The primitive individual does not want "trouble," but once he has it he may do things that are not so irrational as they are unwise. Fortunately, once such an individual is contained by juvenile officers, he will submit to whatever punishment or fine is imposed, although he will complain bitterly about how the "little guy" never has a chance. In some cases, playing cat-and-mouse games with law officials is an acceptable pleasure in itself until he is finally caught. In any case, confrontation requires a straightforward approach like that one would use to discipline a "bad child." In many ways, the primitive adolescent is behaving as a "bad child" and not as an actual delinquent or a disturbed individual. Interestingly, the primitive adolescent often has an acute sense of fairness and justice. His conception of justice may be simplistic and unrealistic for successful adherence to the law, but he often is a law-abiding citizen at heart.

These individuals are most likely to carry their discontinuity into adulthood, and many never advance to a higher and more mature level of behavior. Education and personal development would help them become effective citizens, but often it is too late to give them this needed help. Meeting their behavior remains essentially a matter of law enforcement and control, rather than treatment or severe punishment.

The primitive and unsocialized syndrome in the adolescent girl. We have mentioned before that the terms *primitive* and *unsocialized* seem extreme as descriptions of particular personality patterns. However, these terms are used in the mental health field to denote a particular symptom cluster. The girl who is reared in a home devoid of appropriate and nurturing responses from parents often develops very primitive behaviors that express this deprivation. Often parents may be punitive and rejecting and not provide the role models or responsible parenting that provides security and love to the young girl. The values in the home may be less than appropriate, with a lack of attention to and motivation toward education and achievement. Parents who demonstrate irresponsibility toward their children, are abusive or negligent, and demonstrate attitudes of negativism toward society do not provide the needed environment for developing socialization in their children.

The young girl raised in such an environment often is negative and resistive to socialization on reaching school age. Her school career may be marked by a lack of learning ability, poor study habits and attitudes, and a lack of self-discipline. She often views teachers as substitute parents and is unable to accept direction or affection from adults. This girl becomes attached to her peer culture and unwilling to give up the security and relationships attendant in a group of approving adolescents. Her goals are primarily immediate and concrete, with little regard for conventional values or standards. She operates on an immediate satisfaction goal orientation and becomes highly agitated when she is blocked from goal attainment. In some ways the primitive and unsocialized girl fits the stereotype that society has of so-called bad girls. Several personal characteristics mark the unsocialized adolescent girl: She often dresses inappropriately, is unkempt, and wears make-up in poor taste; or she may wear none at all and adopt a natural, no-bra look or other appearances that tend to be seductive and counterculture. Her tastes run to the garish and are typical of the poorer socioeconomic background from which she comes. The unsocialized girl presents a particularly difficult problem for law enforcement officers and treatment personnel in correctional institutions. With her street-wise attitude and deeply ingrained behavioral patterns, she is not likely to be helped easily. Like the unsocialized boy, she is not so much a delinquent as she is subcultural. Like the boy, she does not intend to break the law, although this may occur. More often, the primitive and unsocialized girl is looking for very basic stimulation, security, love, and rather simple things in life. It is interesting that many of these girls, like the neurotic girl, do place high value on family and children, although they are often less than prepared to provide any better conditions for children than they had themselves. Paralleling the culturally patterned welfare family that makes a living on welfare, the unsocialized girl is likely to eventually drift into a marriage that resembles that of her parents. Her developmental level in education and language is similar to that of a young child.

The unsocialized girl must be treated with objectivity, firmness, and simplicity, for her world is uncomplicated, and she is unable to accept personal responsibility for her behavior. Usually incarceration, if it is to be effective, should be accompanied by long-term counseling and guidance that the law enforcement agencies are unable to provide. The various community agencies, including welfare, family services, mental health clinics, and private facilities, do not usually offer these girls the long-term treatment or assistance that they require. It is not that these agencies do not want or try to aid these girls. Rather, the girl is incarcerated and given some treatment, but, because of the inability of the courts to retain her indefinitely, she returns to the streets to live in the only way she knows how. This is her way of life, and it is as strong for her as the normal middle-class culture is for the typical adolescent.

If our discussion does not offer much hope for the primitive and unsocialized adolescent, it is because it would be less than realistic to suggest that mental health or correctional treatment programs are usually successful with these girls. The struggle is not so much to change a girl as it is a struggle against the entire economically disadvantaged subculture. Certainly poverty is not predictive of delinquency, but it adds a large weight to the scale of probability that an individual will, under certain circumstances, become unable to deal with the larger culture. Only through community action programs, economic and vocational programs, and social action programs can the effects of poverty and deviance be altered. These programs, as most law enforcement officers know, are often too dependent on an apathetic public that is less concerned with why girls become delinquent than it is with the termination of already established delinquent behavior patterns.

The follower

The follower syndrome in the adolescent boy. Another behavioral reaction to discontinuity may be that of immature, infantile, and dependent behavior. Many boys, particularly those who have never been athletically inclined or able to develop other socially valued skills, spend their childhood years engaging in somewhat isolated roles. These children often depend on adults or other peers for more guidance and encouragement than do children who are more or less self-directed and independent. The boy who is a follower is not always a boy who has difficulties in adolescent development, but for those who do experience difficulty, adolescence can be an awesome experience. Like girls, most boys desire acceptance and recognition in their peer group and from adults. The normal child and adolescent form peer relationships even when they have no outstanding skills or social attributes. These individuals are very typical adolescents who do average work in school and follow through with the requirements of social belonging and personal responsibilities.

However, at the fringe of most groups of children, there are individuals who desire social participation and acceptance but are unable to exhibit behaviors that gain them such participation. These boys often are the clinging children who look to others for reinforcement and encouragement. In elementary school these children are somewhat protected because social expectations are less critical, and they can usually gain adequate support from adults around them in order to fit, at least minimally, into the group. On entering adolescence, some of these boys find less support and concern from both teachers and peers. Their adolescent peers are struggling for their own recognition and identity and are less willing to be concerned with the problems of other individuals. The dependent follower is met, therefore, with an increasing dilemma. How does one find a shoulder to lean on when everyone is suddenly more concerned with themselves than with others? The adults in the adolescent's world also seem different from the nurturing and attentive elementary school teachers. The secondary school teacher is often more concerned with accomplishment on the part of adolescents, and less time is spent on personal needs.

Early adolescence is marked by the increased social needs of individuals, and competition for attention and status often becomes more acute. Many dependent boys do find a teacher, another lost student, or some adult in their world to whom they can attach themselves so that they do not become overly upset by the social games of the adolescent group. Many of these boys desire social acceptance and want to belong to a special group of their own, but the only alternative may be to join one of the "out" groups, made up of students who often welcome followers in order to provide for their own need to lead, to gain social importance outside of the normal social group, and to gain support for their own rebellious and hostile feelings toward authority. The dependent follower finds strength and status in being one of a group displaying aggressive attitudes toward the mainstream of social activity in the school. These boys, basically dependent and helpless on their own, feel capable and independent under the leadership and status of the "out" group. The relationship between the aggressive "out" group leader and his dependent followers is one that provides for the needs of both. The "out" group leader cannot be accepted into normal groups of adolescents; the follower also cannot find acceptance in such groups. As a result, the "out" group relationship may become very strong, for the survival of both leader and follower is dependent on its working. When such a group becomes involved with juvenile law, the boys will be quite resistive to confrontation. These boys are not maintaining a relationship simply to have friends or participate in a social group; their relationships meet very basic needs of security, safety, and nurturance. Without the group, they might be unable to function at all. The aggressive or deviant acts of the group become expressions of a disturbed group personality, representing tremendous deficiencies in all the boys involved. For them, there is nothing to lose and everything to gain. This can be a very dangerous group of boys, for in no other group do we find the tendency for individuals to influence others in negative ways. This relationship is the core of adolescent gang and mob behavior. The boys often lose themselves in the euphoria of belonging, finally, to a group in which they have personal status, alliance, and strength.

The group comes to represent even more important values than those of the boy's family. At a time when boys are already struggling for separation from the authority of the family, the group may actually provide, not an individual rebellion, but an irrational and aggressive group rebellion in which the boy becomes lost. His negative reaction to authority and the family is played out through the group to the extent that he may not be held accountable for his behavior. He is simply acting as part of a group, and it is the group that is responsible, while the boy is merely lost and helpless within it. This setting provides the sometimes surprising potential for group violence and aggression that culminates in some shocking crime or act. Since each individual becomes totally committed to the group, the group assumes an actual identity of its own. The individual must follow the group; his own personal responsibility is no longer important as he acts in anonymity.

Officers faced with such groups must react quickly and effectively, since the group can respond in ways unexpected of adolescents. There are few situations in which extreme caution is more important than when dealing with an adolescent group composed of deviant leaders and dependent, follower boys. The group must be confronted quickly when breaking the law, and the individuals must be separated as soon as possible. These boys, once separated from their leader and the group, often yield quickly, since they do not have the responsibility or the courage to "go it alone."

Aside from the leader of the group, who may be a rebel, tend toward psychopathic behavior, or be an aggressive, neurotic individual, the boys often are dependent followers. The families and teachers of the dependent boys are highly responsible for their behavior, since these are boys who, throughout their school careers, have often exhibited the needs of a follower. The adults in the individual boy's life, unimpressed with his needs when he was younger, must focus on these needs at this time, for without such assistance each boy will eventually return to the streets and to the only groups from which he can gain needed security and status. It is important for the juvenile officer and the boy's parents to recognize this behavioral syndrome, since inappropriate reactions from adults are frequent. It seems logical to approach the somewhat dependent boy who is in trouble by stating in what way his behavior is unacceptable and advising that he had best "get things together now or else." Parents often confront the boy with much hostility and disappointment and even rejection. The boy's needs cannot be satisfied by this kind of reaction. His needs are acceptance, limits, reassurance, and much help in setting personal goals. He should be assigned to a counselor in school for support and guidance. Attention should be given to assure that he finds activities and groups in which to participate where he can feel accepted and thus avoid the need to associate with the "out" group. Too often, this does not happen, and the boys return to the streets, where their continuing adolescent growth will be fostered within the deviant culture, resulting in chronic and permanent isolation from and rejection by normal social groups. Fortunately, these boys are often very receptive to help when it comes before their pattern of behavior becomes too hopelessly involved with the "out" group. This is also a group in which the juvenile officer can successfully intervene, since the absence of a leader often demoralizes the group for some period of time. Group behavior and dealing with adolescent groups will be discussed in Chapter 3.

The follower syndrome in the adolescent girl. Women are often thought of as followers by men. However, in groups of women, as in groups of men, there are those who lead and instigate, and those who follow. It is often the more aggressive girl who becomes involved in criminal behavior. However, many delinquent groups have their girl followers, more in the sense of dependency on their male friends than of a behavioral syndrome. Thus, there are general cultural tendencies to teach girls to be followers, to be dependent, and to submit to male leadership. However, as stated before, there are girls who assume leadership roles in their groups. The girls who become leaders often present the most problems for the juvenile officer, since the follower girls, whether following a boy or another girl, are still follower types. There is a stronger tendency in our culture to reinforce followership in girls than in boys. The dependent, follower girl is often more accepted than the follower boy in that *all* boys are expected to be leaders, aggressive, and dominant. There is a tendency to view follower girls as healthier than follower boys. This is not true, although a girl can appear mentally and socially healthier and still be a follower.

The follower syndrome of deviant behavior in the adolescent girl includes all of the characteristics of the follower boy, even though the girl is subject to a cultural bias favoring this kind of behavior. The follower girl can be one who has a poor self-image, who aspires to some sort of aggressive role, or who desires a protective and nurturing group, like the follower boy. The girl who is unable to actualize her own independence can use the group to find strength and acceptance to compensate for her own deficiencies. The group becomes a haven, a means of avoiding development of her own skills and capacities.

Like the follower boy, the follower girl can become aggressive when in the company of the group. Her frustrations may be even more pronounced than those of the boy who is dependent in that the girl may have been "put down," or placed in a submissive role, much of her life, whereas the follower boy may have been encouraged to be a leader. These differing sex-stereotyped expectations can lead to very different psychosocial results with the boy or girl follower. The boy is attempting to live up to cultural expectations, whereas the girl is trying to live down cultural expectations.

Summary

These general descriptions attempt to provide some differentiation between the various personality patterns of adolescent boys and girls who become involved in delinquent acts. A summary of the major characteristics of each syndrome may be of value for the police officer. Although individual characteristics may vary in some degree as an effect of sex, the following characteristics apply to both boys and girls.

ADOLESCENT ADJUSTMENT REACTION

1. History of adequate behavioral adjustment and social interaction with peers.
2. Adequate adjustment in school before adolescence.
3. History of stable home and family structure.
4. Abrupt change in behavior over a relatively short period of time, correlating with the onset of adolescence.
5. Maintenance of adequate peer relationships with occasional periods of withdrawal.
6. Possible sudden change in nature of peer membership from typical adolescent friends to those with some history of deviance.
7. Good response to therapy, counseling, or adult intervention outside the home.
8. Eventual readjustment following behavioral difficulties.

THE REBEL

1. History of adequate to poor behavioral adjustment and social interaction with peers.
2. Adequate to minimal adjustment in school, with negativism and resistance increasing with approach of adolescence.
3. Tendency to question, to challenge, and to attempt to change rules or expectations of adults.
4. History of home situation in which aggression is either encouraged or allowed without adequate limits.
5. Increasing attempts to find and recruit supporters (followers) as adolescent period begins and ensues.
6. Tendency toward intellectualization and idealism.
7. Poor response to therapy and counseling or any authority that attempts to contain or inhibit.
8. Demands for decreased restrictions from adults and authority.

THE NEUROTIC ADOLESCENT

1. History of poor adjustment and peer interaction and difficulties learning to cope with school environment.
2. History of physical, psychosomatic complaints, possible school phobia, and periods of illness resulting in absence from school.

45

3. Difficulty in school subjects often suspected to be caused by a lack of motivation, interest, or involvement.
4. Tendency to be a scapegoat of groups or friends in school.
5. Tendency to be fearful, anxiety-prone, nonaggressive, negative, and dependent on others.
6. Parents who appear unconcerned or who are overly punitive and authoritarian.
7. Failure-oriented in school and community, making successful participation in groups difficult or impossible.
8. Tendency to blame others, environment, or situation for personal failure.

THE SOCIOPATHIC ADOLESCENT

1. History of poor parenting, management, and probable neglect of basic needs and love within the home.
2. History of poor school adjustment and learning.
3. Limited skill development in school and poor achievement.
4. Tendency to attempt to manipulate, to evade rules, to be expedient, and to seek ways of avoiding responsibility or accountability.
5. Negativism toward authority and association with other students who are the "outs" in the school and community.
6. Early involvement in drug use, infractions of the law, and antisocial behavior.
7. Inability to share warmth, to nurture or accept nurturance, and a lack of ongoing peer relationships.
8. Early tendency to attempt to manipulate or develop strategies of control over peers.

THE PRIMITIVE AND UNSOCIALIZED ADOLESCENT

1. History of poor home conditions and lack of adequate parenting, supervision, and limit setting.
2. Lack of regard for learning or a lack of responsibility for school achievement.
3. Low achievement and intellectual abilities as perceived by teachers or in psychological testing.
4. Impulsive behavior, with an inability to see relationships between behavior and consequences.
5. Tendency to act out feelings and aggression to obtain personal needs or satisfaction.
6. Tendency to avoid rules, verbal interaction, and interpersonal responsibility.
7. Poor occupational goals and a lack of definition of personal direction.
8. Willingness to join peer groups in which excitement and aggression are promised.

THE FOLLOWER

1. History of marginal adjustment in school, an inability to form peer relationships, and withdrawal tendencies.
2. Poor parental acceptance, lack of nurturing, or even authoritarian parents who tend toward rejecting attitudes; parent may be overly protective and reinforce a lack of independence in the child at an early age.
3. Early indicators of dependence on others, on authority, or on an environment that offers security.
4. Poor school achievement and an inability to complete assignments without assistance.

5. High degree of deference to peers, authority, or rules.
6. Poor physical status and difficulties in general physical skills.
7. Potential acts of passive aggressiveness in late elementary school and/or early adolescence.
8. Increasing withdrawal and avoidance of responsibility during adolescence.

SOCIOLOGY VERSUS PSYCHOLOGY

When an adolescent becomes delinquent, many authorities in the mental health fields often disagree about the causal factors for the adolescent's behavior. The psychologist emphasizes the pathology of the individual's personality structure, whereas the sociologist looks on the child's environment, his culture or group and peers, and the general conditions surrounding the child's life as causal factors. The latter factors provide a general viewpoint that describes behavior without suggesting that an individual is either primarily suffering from psychologically or sociologically related conditions. A problem in the professional study of deviant behavior is the difficulty of summarizing or indicating specific factors as most significant in the behavior of any individual. We believe that problematic behavior in any individual is based on a lack of adaptive skill. Adaptation to a particular set of conditions within a social group requires not only the capacity to learn coping behaviors but also the opportunity. Children spend the first years of their lives in environments that vary in the opportunity to learn successful adaptive behavior.

There are certain genetic and prenatal conditions that may predispose an individual to learning specific behaviors, adaptive or maladaptive. Physiological health, adequate nutrition, maternal care, establishment of trust and caring, and the early opportunity to learn specific social and intellectual or language skills all contribute to the individual's adaptive behavior potential. The interaction between early childhood and genetic factors determines the direction an individual will take. Children with poor physiological health, specific genetic or prenatal defects, and even poor early social environments can learn to cope and grow into adequate adults. Conversely, some children who come from adequate early environments and who are physiologically healthy may not learn successful coping behavior.

It is important to recognize that the interaction between individual potential and the environment forms the critical core of behavioral outcomes. One cannot describe an individual without recognizing both innate capacity and social environment, since the measure of an individual's adjustment will be dependent on both. Any of us, even after an initial period of successful adult adjustment, may become incompetent under certain conditions. There are critical times in child and adolescent development when certain language, motor, perceptual, and personality skills

47

appear to be learned most effectively. A number of conditions can alter this timing and render later development less adaptive than it might have been. Depending on the severity of such difficulties, the individual's later adjustment may be affected.

It might be suggested that the earlier in one's life that some sort of deviance is experienced, the less potential there will be for deviance at a later time. In later chapters that deal with adolescent behavior, the reader should keep in mind that cause and effect may be difficult to establish, but the key to change in the adolescent is learning adaptation and coping skills. How successful we are in assisting the individual or how success-fully he works toward change goals is never totally predictable and often responsive to both personality and social factors that may be beyond our control at any moment. In the following chapters we will discuss some aspects of delinquent behavior and the crimes with which they are associ-ated. These crimes and behaviors will be related back to the behavioral clusters we have presented here. Of course, these must be generalizations that should never be used as a final means of classifying or treating an adolescent who needs help. The classifications only provide general pa-rameters for looking at behavior to help the officer formulate a framework for understanding the adolescent's behavior. The terms used in our classifications, although slanted toward psychological terminology, are meant to function as sociopersonality classifications implying the in-teractive potential of personality and social disorders. The individual with personality difficulties will find difficulties in his social interactions with peers and adults. The child who has not learned adequate social skills or who comes from a cultural environment in which adequate par-enting was not provided will probably develop personality difficulties.

ADDITIONAL READINGS

Clarizio, H., & McCoy, G. *Behavior disorders in school-aged children.* San Francisco: Chan-dler, 1970.

Cressey, D., & Ward, D. *Delinquency, crime, and social process.* New York: Harper & Row, 1969.

Grinder, R. *Studies in adolescence.* New York: Macmillan, 1975.

Holland, M. *Psychology.* Lexington, Mass.: D. C. Heath, 1974.

Long, N., Morse, W., & Newman, R. *Conflict in the classroom.* Belmont, Calif.: Wadsworth, 1971.

McCandless, B. R. *Adolescents: Behavior and development.* Hinsdale, Ill.: Dryden Press, 1970.

Rodes, W., & Tracey, M. *A study of child variance.* Ann Arbor, Mich.: University of Michi-gan Press, 1972.

CHAPTER 3

THE NATURE OF GROUP PSYCHOLOGY

We can be grouped and classified,
But each of us is unique.

49

Much of the literature on adolescent development involves the nature of individual behavior relative to social groups. Just as important and often excluded from such information are the effects of group behavior on the individual. This aspect of adolescent behavior is as significant to law enforcement as the behavior of the individual. Often, the officer must deal not only with individuals but with individuals who are part of an organized and cohesive group. If the officer is not aware of the psychology of both individual and group behavior, he is at a disadvantage.

THE FUNCTION OF THE ADOLESCENT GROUP

Adolescence is the final stage of human development before adulthood. Adults are primarily social beings who function within community and family structures. From the social group adults gain status, recognition, security, economic independence, and acceptance. Adolescence is a proving ground for many social and family behaviors that will be important to eventual entrance of the individual into organized community life. Many adolescents spend most of their time in some sort of group, experiencing and practicing behaviors that will assist them in adjusting to family and community life. Under optimal conditions, this period of practice is fruitful and provides the insight and understanding each individual needs to become a responsible household head and citizen. There are many adolescents, however, who do not gain adequate or appropriate group experience for eventual entrance into the mainstream of social behavior.

Earlier discussions have pointed out that adolescents need the group for the establishment of individual identity and social belonging. Although this need is significant in the development of the individual, there is no assurance that the identity which a particular group reinforces will be an appropriate one. Since the adolescent needs the group for establishment of independence from his family, deviant groups may provide as adequate a mechanism as normal social groups. The difficulty results from the consequences of belonging to and identifying with a deviant group. Some of the major provisions of group membership are the following:

1. A peer age-specific group for identification that holds goals, interests, and values similar to those of the individual seeking group membership.
2. A refuge and sympathetic substitute family that satisfies the individual's present level of maturity and personal interest or concern.
3. A supportive group for the individual's needs in developing independence from adults and the authority culture, establishing

personal reference values appropriate for the age of the individual, and opportunities for learning or obtaining new information important in establishing personal autonomy.

4. The interpersonal courage to practice relationships and take risks in attempting sexual behaviors that the individual alone might be fearful of attempting.
5. A reference group for testing and learning new values for personal and interpersonal behaviors.
6. A social group in which pairing relationships can be practiced along with relating both to one's own partner and to other individuals in pairing relationships.
7. A basic and secure reference group for obtaining feedback on one's own personal values, characteristics, and capabilities.
8. Practice in sex role behaviors appropriate to boys and girls that will eventuate in adult sex role models.
9. A reference and experimental group in which the individual can develop personal philosophies of religious beliefs, moral standards, and initial life goals.
10. A feeling of group unity and belonging that will eventuate in adult social group membership and participation in occupational, family, and community behavior.

The foregoing group membership outcomes represent tremendously important factors in personal development during adolescence. If the individual is successful in obtaining group membership in which all of these can be experienced, then the transition into adulthood will be successful. Although these behaviors may eventuate in adult adjustment into social groups, the nature of the group can have a profound influence on the nature of that adjustment. An individual can learn group social behaviors in adolescence that provide for adjustment into deviant or criminal adult groups just as easily as behaviors that result in adjustment into more or less normal adult social groups. Significantly, the way in which the group influences the individual at this critical stage results in a personal growth and orientation that may be difficult or impossible to alter. Intervention in deviant group identification, therefore, is extremely important.

PARTICIPATION IN DEVIANT GROUPS

It must be realized that there are few, if any, adolescents who really desire to become criminals or to enter deviant groups. Usually, the adolescent who is involved in deviant group membership would rather belong to a normal group if this were possible. For this reason, the younger adolescent who is beginning to identify with such groups usually is still receptive to some way out. Frequently, however, the individual is stereotyped and cast in the role of an "out" once he enters such a group, and parents, teachers, and peers are quite unforgiving when this occurs. The probability is strong that negative reactions from adults and peers to deviant group identification and participation tend to force the boy or girl more deeply into such group membership. Furthermore, there is little doubt that teachers could identify and alter such behavior early in adolescence, if there were interest and programs were available. In the sixth, seventh, and eighth grades, all of the signs, such as truancy, poor school grades, and negative attitudes, are well known to the school. Too often the parents and the school waste these years attempting to place blame, rather than initiating effective programs.

In reviewing, it becomes evident that some of the influences of group behavior become so strong that individuals appear lost and unable to alter their behavior, even though they may feel guilty and desire escape. The group develops a personality that subordinates its members. In all groups, whether civic, fraternal, religious, or political, there is an overall group identity that is greater than the members of the group. The creed, laws, or philosophy of the group tends to become a collective reflection of the members. Hence, members of certain groups are expected to behave in specific ways because of their particular group membership. This is, of course, a significant aspect of stereotyping and bias in our culture. It is often said that black kids initiate racial disturbance, that specific religious groups cannot be trusted, that all Boy Scouts are good kids, or that men who are Jaycees are community-minded and outstanding citizens. Members of such groups, although they may vary greatly as individuals, tend to behave in ways that they and others expect of the group. In this manner, the general group role and identity become part of the individual's identity and, in fact, can cause significant changes in his behavior. For example, the boy who belongs to the Boy Scouts may be a much more considerate and responsible boy while engaging in Scout activities than he would otherwise be. To this extent, then, the group's personality is greater than the sum of its members.

Group personality and identity are very powerful social motivators and shapers of individual behavior. Men in combat will often perform heroic acts because of their group membership identity that they would never be capable of doing without the group association. In fact, individuals may even commit acts that destroy them because of this identification with the group. Such energy and strength as a consequence of group membership become a significant aspect of dealing with an individual who is participating in an organized group. If an officer is confronted with such a group, he is at a tremendous disadvantage, since individuals in the group may be willing to commit acts that far exceed the individual officer's commitment to counterbehavior.

Group formation

Groups develop in stages. Individuals may come together because of some common cause and form a group, either accidentally or for some vague and temporary goal. For example, a particular teacher may alienate several students in his class. Initially, these students may have little in common, but they may eventually develop a feeling of mutual identification because of their individual suffering under the teacher. None of these youths may have been specifically looking for group membership, but during the class period they may become increasingly aware of their mutual dilemma and slowly begin to identify with each other. This initial mutuality in suffering or cause is significant enough to begin the group formation process. Similar situations can occur because of mutual interest in community activity, athletics, or in other harmless pursuits. The essential result is that the youths find themselves in a situation involving some sort of mutual interest or problem. Because of the natural adolescent need for support from peers, individuals may initiate a relationship that quickly expands to include four, six, or eight others. It is interesting to note that adolescent as well as adult groups tend to reach a maximum size of about eight to ten members, with the ideal being closer to eight. This ideal number holds for informal groups rather than formal organizations such as Scout troops, athletic teams, or school clubs, and it is the informal group that becomes the mainstay of adolescent behavior. Adolescent informal groups that exceed five to eight members are usually short-term groups and are exceedingly unstable. The informal group, since it has no formalized organizational structure, tends to develop in ways that are unpredictable; however, it may be a very cohesive group. Five to eight individuals will not participate in mutual interaction for very long before an informal leader emerges. In this kind of group, leadership potential is exhibited by one or more members through risk-taking behaviors, aggression, dominance, or some special skill or knowledge. When these talents are recognized by the group, most members will usually submit to the dominance of the emerging leader. This requires some time of association and may involve competition between two or more members for group acceptance of their leadership role.

During the initial stages of group formation and before the establishment of an actual leader, the group is somewhat unstable, and intervention is more easily accomplished. This is why teachers and juvenile officers can sometimes break up a group easily at the outset if they are able to recognize the absence of general group cohesion or of an actual leader. Sometimes teachers will take a "wait and see" approach that allows time for a leader to emerge. Once the leader has emerged, the group begins a period of relative euphoria and increased identification with each other. At this stage of group formation, however, they are not particularly well organized, and often an individual will drop out of the group. There may be much complaining and resistance, but such a separation can more easily be accomplished at this stage. During this stage, the members of the group spend much time together in more or less aimless association, simply learning more about each other and enjoying the initial feeling of belonging that comes from acceptance into a new group of friends. Depending on the situation and the amount of time the group can spend together, this period of increased socialization may last for several weeks or months. Following this period, the group eventually builds toward what may be called *task orientation*. When the group enters this stage, the members begin looking for a purpose, a goal, or a task for the group. At this point, the leader begins to emerge as an organizational leader who directs the group toward some specific goal. Often this goal may be, if the group has a deviant orientation, a criminal act or, at least, antisocial acts. The group assumes a name such as Hell's Angels or the East Side Crusaders. Usually, the labels that the boys attach to their groups provide a general orientation for the emerging group personality. Along with this development, certain group rules for membership are also formed that provide the guidelines for group membership and assure commitment to the tasks of the group. If the tasks are oriented toward criminal acts, then the rules for group membership will be appropriate. For example, a new member may be expected to shoplift, to perform specified antisocial acts in school or against his family, or to commit other such acts to prove his loyalty and worthiness to the group. Thus, the delinquent group reaches the final stage of formation.

Group personality and membership

Once the group has formed, the boy becomes immersed in the group personality and will perform acts that he might not have the courage to attempt alone. Although in this case the goals of the group are deviant, the same process occurs for a normal adolescent or adult group. It is the nature and purpose of the group that set it apart from other groups and make it more or less acceptable. Once the group has reached the final level of formation, it becomes quite resistive to external intervention. One of the strongest cohesive forces in the group is that of threat from the outside. Whenever a group is threatened by an outside force, it tends to intensify its cohesiveness and defensiveness to levels that may motivate the members to perform nearly irrational acts in order to protect the group. When a group is confronted by the juvenile officer, the cohesive force is set into motion. Therefore, it is important that juvenile officers attempt to intervene in such groups with as little initial force as possible to avoid this intensification process. Separation of group members is of utmost importance, and methods used in confrontation of a cohesive and organized group must either be extremely forceful, so as to disperse the members quickly, or subtle and nonaggressive.

Certainly, it is important to identify group leaders and attempt to work into the group through the leader. It is often thought that separation of the leader from the group will tend to defuse and disorganize the group. Unfortunately, this is only true in certain stages of group formation. If the group is well organized and cohesive, separation of the leader will simply stimulate the emergence of a new leader, almost at once, making confrontation with the group extremely difficult. Moreover, if the group is to disband, then they will have to be prevented from interaction over an extended period of time, which is often quite difficult.

In summary, the individual's group membership is of utmost importance, and adults involved with boys who belong to "out" groups should constantly take into account each individual member in the group. Parents and teachers should be alert to group behavior as early as possible and attempt to determine the health or deviance of the particular group to which a boy is attracted. These brief comments on group behavior are extremely important for discussion and training programs in the juvenile field.

GROUP BEHAVIOR IN LOWER-CLASS "GANGS"

Whereas group behavior is very important for the adolescent in developing identity and social skills, it also often performs many functions that are more basic and not unlike those of the family. As we have stated, the adolescent group is realized as the individual is seeking a substitute "family" away from home. Within this "family" the adolescent can begin to formulate his own separate identity and practice those behaviors that will allow him to learn effective interpersonal and social behaviors. However, for adolescents from various segments of the population, the adolescent group may turn from a social group into a "gang." The term *gang* is used by school and legal professionals almost exclusively to indicate that a certain group is in some manner deviant. Often the "gang" is a group of lower-class adolescents who in some way threaten and intimidate the community and school.

W. B. Miller (1958, cited in Kauffman, 1977) hypothesizes that lower-class culture is a generating environment for gang delinquency. In recent years, however, there has been an increase in gang delinquency in the affluent middle class. However, there are distinctive differences between the lower-class and middle-class delinquent groups that should be recognized by police officers. Although both groups tend to form in the manner outlined in our previous discussion, the motivation and behavior of the two groups may be quite different.

According to Miller, lower-class society focuses on concerns and values of its own that are quite different from those of the middle class. Many professionals in social science today are concerned that the lower class is growing and that their values and concerns may contribute extensively to the growing problem of crime. Miller states that the focus of concern in the lower class is in the following areas:

trouble Emphasis on law-violating behavior versus law-abiding behavior.

toughness Physical prowess combined with "masculinity," lack of sentimentality, and exploitative attitudes toward women, or behavior that might be interpreted as weakness.

smartness The ability to "outwit," "con," "take," or "dupe" others and to avoid being "taken" by others.

excitement Periods of intense excitement breaking an overall rhythm of boredom and routine.

fate The belief that luck rather than personal control or decision controls one's life.

autonomy The desire to be free from constraint and control by authority, mixed with the wish to be cared for.[1]

The lower-class gang provides the mechanism for expressing and acting out these concerns. In order to be accepted into such a gang, the adolescent must exhibit behaviors that identify him as a member of this group. The gang provides the social milieu in which these concerns can be actualized. Because these concerns are expressed not only as behavioral characteristics but as values, such a group becomes very difficult for the community to control or alter.

This value structure provides an anti-intellectual atmosphere for the adolescent in which feelings, pleasures, and action substitute for logic, achievement, and conformity. Such a group may be compared with the Robin Hood syndrome of the oppression of the good guys by the affluent bad guys. It is a counterculture where intellectualism is absent and "mob" behavior exists, in which the members of the group not only find mutual empathy for their economic and social repression but reinforcement in their fight against the "good" people of the society.

Because of the pervasive social and economic structure of this subcultural group, alteration of the individuals becomes extremely difficult, and they represent a significant threat to middle-class society. Law enforcement, representing the middle-class value system, comes headlong into conflict with this group. This group might be composed of individuals who represent the worst aspect of the primitive and unsocialized syndrome. Volumes of material have been written about how to assist these adolescents and the entire subcultural group, but political and economic realities dictate that real change for such individuals will have to be founded in dramatic change in our entire system of social structure. This is not a likely probability from a historical viewpoint. The following discussion presents overall goals that law enforcement officers must keep in mind when dealing with these gangs.

Punishment versus rehabilitation

The subculture gang member is often an individual who has never been socialized in the traditional sense. He has developed in an alien culture and therefore cannot be "rehabilitated" since he has never been "habilitated" in the first place. Psychiatric and psychological treatment strategies have been somewhat ineffective in altering an individual's total personality and social conditioning. For this group of individuals, rehabilitation is often ineffective because of the inability of social treatment to profoundly reshape the personality structure of an individual after he or she reaches adolescence or adulthood, when much of the personality pattern is set.

However, punishment often tends to serve only an inhibiting function, preventing the individual from acting on his beliefs as long as the punishment or control is exercised. Once he is released from detention, he will probably turn once more to his cultural counterparts, and, in order to be reincorporated into his social group, he will have to again act out in his basic pattern of behavior. Often punishment even increases his resistance and determination to maintain his alienated belief patterns.

One would like to offer the police officer some note of optimism, some thread of possibility that such individuals could be changed. However, in large urban areas this culture is as much a social and political reality as the middle class. Containment is often the major goal of law enforcement. Prostitution, taking from the rich, and professional crime become part or the whole of many individual's life styles, enabling them to survive in their economic and social environment. At present, there are no significant developments in law enforcement that provide the police officer with effective means of altering the conditions and the environment in which such behavior is developed. The police role becomes one of enforcement. Only political and economic change will get at the basis for the existence of chronically poor Americans and eventually alter their plight.

Perhaps one of the most pervasive and difficult problems facing our culture today is that of the lower class and all of its associated difficulties. The formation of teenage gangs is becoming a "normal" adolescent process within this group. The gangs provide the means by which an adolescent, who may have seldom seen his father or known the typical, middle-class family structure, finds for the first time a feeling of belonging, cohesion, acceptance, and purpose. These personal needs are met within the gang, and their satisfaction provides an almost impregnable defense against attempts from the outside to change the members. What the gang believes becomes right because of group verification. This is not a group of disturbed, criminal individuals; rather, it is a group of individuals with a different viewpoint from that of the mainstream of society. Their behaviors form the Robin Hood syndrome.

The alteration of gangs or specific individuals within such groups requires long-term intervention. Social action agencies have made some progress working within the community along with law enforcement agencies in assisting families and individuals toward a more appropriate life style and membership in society. However, these programs are costly, and there never seem to be quite enough for increasing numbers of gangs and alienated individuals in our culture. Confinement and programs of rehabilitation, although often discouragingly ineffective, do help many individuals toward a better adjustment when they return to the community. Punishment, in all of its forms, provides a measure of restriction for the gang members but in itself does not alter behavior; it merely stops behavior temporarily. However, imprisonment may at least provide the opportunity to attempt rehabilitation of the individual. Thus, although our attempts to change individuals in such gangs is constantly thwarted by the larger social causes of the problem, we must continue to attempt to develop programs that provide change potential for these individuals.

Gangs are becoming more vocal and active in schools, work programs, and the communities. School officials around the country have found an increasing number of gang behaviors that tend to disrupt the school. However, this is truer in urban areas and not a general concern across the country. In the late 1960's and early 1970's, many students were rebelling against the "system," and there were many confrontations between students and school officials. That portion of the adolescent culture has not continued its crusade to change the system; in the mid-1970's, we saw a rapid disappearance of the idealistic confrontations of the recent past. Although the middle- and upper-class adolescents are withdrawing from their attempts to change the system, another problem is left behind that has been growing all the while: the lower-class adolescent gang. This group has found much support during recent years for the idea that society is wrong, that schools and the law are on the side of economics and not justice, and that there is no other way to survive than to confront and "beat" the system.

Aggression and counteraggression are escalating behaviors that usually result in total destruction of one or both forces. The only alternative to such results is compromise, that is, developing strategies for living together. The confrontation of lower-class society and the middle class is such a situation, strange as it might seem. The middle class is not

58

willing to assist the poor and underprivileged in ways that will make it possible for them to survive. Society works toward restriction and containment of this segment of the population. This situation breeds further resentment and hostilities. School officials find the adolescent gangs an increasing threat. At present, aggression and compromise are both being used to control the situation. It is not a police problem but a problem of culture and people. Unfortunately, society is willing to let and even demands that the police solve the problem: use force to stop crime. This already has bred and will breed more crime in that force is being used to control a segment of the population that is discriminated against.

GANGS OF AFFLUENCY

The lower-class gangs are an increasing threat to society, but the middle class also has its problem in controlling the adolescent group. An increasing problem with middle-class gangs has begun to emerge in the last decade. The middle-class gang that becomes involved in criminal behavior is a very different group from its lower-class counterpart. The group members tend to be individuals who have been acceptable members of the middle class until adolescence. Middle-class delinquency is sometimes a one-shot affair in which the adolescent, for a variety of reasons, may plan and execute some sort of illegal act. Other delinquents, according to Elkind,[2] are often individuals with psychological difficulties who require psychiatric rather than legal treatment. However, it seems that the majority of middle-class delinquents are individuals who are chronically in trouble, and their problems are rooted in family interaction difficulties. Elkind believes that there is a social contract between middle-class parents and children that implies that the parent will take responsibility for the emotional well-being of the child. In exchange, the adolescent sacrifices some of his freedom, obeys rules, and remains loyal to the parents' standards.

Often the middle-class delinquent is an individual who feels his parents are not living up to their part of the contract. He feels that he is not loved, that they do not attempt to understand him, or that they do not care about his needs. Of course, all of these feelings are often associated with temporary periods during adolescence. In cases where there is parental neglect of the adolescent, he may look elsewhere to obtain the love and acceptance he does not find at home. Because he is somewhat angry and resentful of his parents and adults in general, the adolescent gang becomes an excellent vehicle for serving both his need for acceptance and status and his need to express hostility toward authority.

The middle-class gang is composed of individuals who are more apt

59

to be directly in conflict with the authority of the middle class than is the lower-class gang. Both groups focus their attention on the middle and upper classes as targets for disgust and conflict, but the motivation of each group is very different. The lower-class delinquent identifies with his social group, which is rejected and oppressed by the middle class. His motivation to "rape" the culture is for material gain, to "pay back a debt owed him," to verify his position of rebellion, and to fight the oppressive forces about him. He seeks pleasure, status, challenge, and power.

The middle-class gang is often seeking thrills also, but its thrill-seeking is often related to a need for status, for experimentation rather than simply for feeling, for engaging in risk-taking behaviors, or for gaining recognition. The middle-class gang member is more likely to be achievement oriented in some way, and he often enjoys competition as opposed to simple confrontation. The middle-class gang member in many ways may be more unpredictable than the lower-class individual, since there may be more pathology in or psychological reasons for his behavior as opposed to social factors. The lower-class gang member accepts the gang as a substitute family, and his identification with the family is often total. His commitment reaches the level of commitment between blood brothers. But the middle-class delinquent is more often an individual who basically is still imbued with middle-class values. He is actively resisting and confronting those values, but he will probably reflect ideas and beliefs of the middle class rather than of the lower class. Often the middle-class delinquent is wrestling with intellectual and emotional dissonance, rather than simply acting out a way of life like the lower-class delinquent. Thus, the middle-class gang member may be less predictable, since the basis for his behavior is founded more in personality factors than in intercultural conflict. It is probable that the middle-class delinquent is more open to change because he is able to readopt an attitude of conformity that, before his difficulties with the law, he exhibited during childhood. The lower-class gang member is less open to change, because he has never conformed or adapted to the middle-class value structure in the first place.

Police response to lower-class gangs must be based on the realization that there is less logic, responsibility, and potential for change than in middle-class society. It will require the use of punishment and force, since language will not be an available mechanism for change. The lower-class delinquent is more apt to act than talk. Conversely, the middle-class delinquent often seeks conflict as an opportunity to express his feelings, to show his need for help, or to dramatize his perception of unfairness in the world. Such an individual is more open to therapy, to group projects and sessions, and to individual support from adults.

REFERENCES

1. Kauffman, J. M. *Characteristics of children's behavior disorders.* Columbus, Ohio: Charles Merrill, 1977.
2. Elkind, D. Middle class delinquency. *Mental Hygiene,* 1967, **51,** 80-84.

ADDITIONAL READINGS

Cartwright, P., & Zander, A. *Group dynamics: Research and theory.* New York: Harper & Row, 1968.

Grinder, R. *Studies in adolescence.* New York: Macmillan, 1975.

Hamachek, D. E. *Encounters with the self.* New York: Holt, Rinehart & Winston, 1971.

Katz, D., & Kahn, R. *The social psychology of organizations.* New York: Wiley, 1966.

Moreno, J. L. *Who shall survive?* New York: Beacon House, 1953.

Napier, R. W., and Gershenfeld, M. K.: *Groups: Theory and experience.* Boston: Houghton Mifflin, 1973.

Sherif, M., & Sherif, C. W. *Social psychology.* New York: Harper & Row, 1969.

CHAPTER 4

THE THINKING ADOLESCENT

If I have to live your way today,
When will my tomorrow come?

One of the greatest mistakes adults make in attempting to understand the adolescent is to assume that the adolescent thinks like an adult or is capable of such thinking but behaves differently. This is far from the actual case, and some understanding of the sequential development of thought processes in adolescence is important if the juvenile officer is to effectively assist individuals who may be having difficulty. Children are not miniature adults, and adolescence is that period of time when the thought process of the child slowly develops, through experience and practice, into the more complex and mature thought process of the adult. There are many factors that contribute to this development, and, just as individual adolescents develop at different rates physically and socially, they vary in their intellectual maturation. Some may still function intellectually below a level that might be expected. Conversely, many adolescents, because of the nature of their cultural background, intellectual ability, and success in learning, develop somewhat mature thinking before the beginning of adolescence. Unfortunately, there are many adults who never develop mature thought processes but remain fixated somewhere between childhood and adulthood. It is of great advantage, therefore, for the juvenile officer and other law enforcement professionals to have some knowledge of the developmental stages of thought process.

Since physical size and maturity are not good indicators of the maturity of an individual's thought processes, an understanding of thought process development is important in responding to the needs and crises of an individual, regardless of his age. Such awareness will not only make it possible to deal more effectively with the offender but will give the officer an additional means of understanding the offender and responding to the situation.

The following examples form an overview of the developmental thought process.

THE ABILITY TO FORM SIMPLE RELATIONSHIP DEDUCTIONS

The child often sees the world in "black and white" terms. Given a certain situation, he will evaluate it in terms of gross generalization and be fairly assured that the conclusion is correct. This is the basis of much prejudice and bias in society. Archie Bunker, in the well-known television series, gives a good example of this kind of thought process in an adult. The following conclusions are examples of how the child or the immature adult or adolescent may view the world:

1. Women are poor drivers. Betty is a woman; therefore, Betty is a poor driver.

2. Black people are good basketball players. Bob is black; therefore, he is a good basketball player.
3. Policemen hassle teenagers. Bill is a policeman; therefore, he will hassle teenagers.
4. Politicians are crooked. Jim is an employee of the city; therefore, he is a crook.
5. Parents don't understand teenagers. I am a teenager; consequently, my parents don't understand me.

These examples give an idea of this illogical thinking. Although the error of this type of thinking might seem obvious, there are important emotional reasons why an individual may resist accepting logic that demonstrates that his conclusions are wrong. In the case of the adolescent who is at this level of thought process development, there is both an illogical thought process and an associated emotional factor that will usually prevent any short-term change in the position that the adolescent takes. Thought process development will be based on the emerging ability of the adolescent to "think" objectively and logically. This development is based on two critical factors: First, his ability to think objectively and logically requires a nonthreatening environment and opportunities to learn that stereotyped beliefs do not always fit the situation. Such a process takes time. Second, his ability to think logically will be influenced greatly by his own personality and attitudes. If he has a good self-concept and is not threatened by the fact that a current belief he holds is in error, he may listen to the new information and, on the basis of the reality before him, change his belief. Conversely, if he has a poor self-concept and is confronted with information that conflicts with what he believes, changing his belief would not only make him feel intellectually inadequate but would further damage his already poor self-concept. As he matures and becomes confident in himself, his ability to think logically will improve. If he is immature and has a poor self-concept, his ability to think logically will be severely hampered. The combination of illogical thinking and unstable self-concept is most often the basis for continuing inappropriate behaviors in adolescence.

When one is confronted with an adolescent who demonstrates illogical thinking as a result of his poor self-image, the following approaches may be of value:

1. Ask questions that stimulate the individual to state his position. Follow these questions, in a nonthreatening way, with objective questions that force the individual to reflect on his behavior and his general position.
2. Give the individual some alternatives to his own position, and ask him if he can explain the seeming contradictions in or exceptions to his position.

3. Clarify for the individual how his position is inappropriate, and explain that other possibilities exist. Assure him that subsequent action, whether arrest or release, is based on the logic of these other alternatives.

4. Proceed with action.

This process will not resolve the problem if the individual is truly immature and emotionally incompetent. However, it will allow the officer to clarify for the individual the basis on which he is acting. In addition, it is this kind of experience that may lead the individual to reassess his position and to begin to make changes. If the individual is incompetent, such an interaction will give the officer more assurance that firm action is the only route to take. If reason fails, then the officer is reduced to using force and threat in order to change the offender's behavior. Although we might like to avoid this action, if logic cannot be used, then the offender cannot be expected to alter his behavior without more punitive action; pain and inconvenience are a universal language. They do not solve the problem, but they impose a temporary constraint on the individual's behavior that may provide an opportunity for him to reflect and eventually develop more reasonable behavior. This is the best that can be done with individuals at this level of thought process development without extensive educational and special service programs. Preferably, such an individual would be placed on probation so that he can be assisted in mental growth over an extended period of time.

The outcome of satisfactory intellectual development is that the individual eventually becomes more objective and situation-specific about his beliefs. For example, although he may recognize that many parents are unable to understand their teenagers, he will understand that not all parents have such difficulty and that each situation will have to be evaluated. This higher level of thinking involves the ability to look at situations and to assess objectively the conclusion based on two or more factors in that particular situation. There is little doubt that immature thinking by adults in this particular area is the basis for much difficulty in understanding adolescents. Adults who are themselves immature make the same generalizations about adolescents that immature adolescents make about adults. This produces a very frustrating environment for police officers who must deal with these types of adolescents and parents. Perhaps even more frustrating are those situations in which the mature adolescent is driven to delinquent behavior because of immature parents.

Because the development of mature thinking requires experience and opportunity to learn new beliefs, adolescents can be very frustrating to parents and other adults as they test out their own emerging ideas and attempt to ascertain what they believe. Many adults react to the questioning adolescent in negative ways. His questions threaten them and cause them to attempt to "put him down" in order to evade his questions. Adolescents who finally reach the more mature levels of thought process begin to pick out the real incongruencies in the adult world. As they continue to mature and explore their world, they often become very idealistic and euphoric with their new intellectual power to evaluate. Suddenly, things they have never questioned become totally absurd. Parents may claim Christianity and then cheat on their taxes, speed on the highway, lie to friends about being sick and unable to attend a party, or simply tell the adolescent to "buzz off" when confronted with their own incongruent behavior. These minor mental confrontations occur between adolescents and parents, police officers, teachers, and other adolescents. Being faced suddenly with a child who now is questioning a long-held belief system can be a very disconcerting experience and requires that the adult be a somewhat developed and mature thinker. The adolescent needs these confrontations, for he is attempting to develop exactly what is desirable, a mature and independent personality.

As the adolescent struggles for clarity in his thought process, adults should attempt to respond with considered answers as to the nature of the adult world and assist the adolescent in gaining an opportunity to obtain information. He will then be able to use the information to develop his own philosophy of life and to determine how he will conduct himself. Attempting to hide adult frailties and forcing the adolescent to conform will simply develop hostility and suspicion and inhibit his mental growth. This does not mean that the adolescent should not learn respect and consideration for authority and adults but that adults should not be threatened by his developing mental ability.

THE ABILITY TO SEE THE EFFECTS OF TWO OR MORE FACTORS ON A RELATED OR UNRELATED THIRD FACTOR

As the adolescent expands his general ability to react to new information without immature and illogical beliefs, an important additional skill emerges. He can now see how his behavior or that of his friends may affect others, although it seems completely independent. It is at this stage that the first real signs of adult consideration and responsibility begin to emerge. The adolescent now realizes that his insistence on going out late at night or acting in certain ways may reflect not only on his family but on his friends. If the adolescent has not reached this state of mental development, he will not be able to understand why his behavior is so important to the juvenile officer or why so many people, including his parents, are constantly imposing limits on his behavior. As he matures, he begins to predict the consequences of his own behavior on more remote situations. For example, it now becomes important to be conscious of one's responsibility as a citizen, rather than simply as a member of a group or family. During this stage, the adolescent can become even more idealistic and join "causes" or movements in order to improve the world. Suddenly, the adolescent feels that his behavior is important and that the individual should develop a self-consciousness that is not only local but national as well. This mental function is also seen in the developing consideration the adolescent displays for his girlfriend, her family, and friends. The adolescent can consider the consequences of his behavior before acting, and, subsequently, he finds less friction in his general life style.

This new awareness is based on continuing experience, developing self-assurance, and slowly emerging feelings of personal responsibility that will eventually become a permanent part of his adult-parent personality. The critical responsibilities of family membership and being a parent are dependent on this developing ability to perceive the relationship of the individual's behavior to somewhat remote events. This will be important in understanding friends and community membership in coming years.

THE ABILITY TO HYPOTHESIZE

With his increasing ability to see remote relationships between various factors, the adolescent's thought process develops into the phase of higher abstract thinking; now he can use several factors to create a new idea or theory. This kind of thinking makes it possible for him to create reasons not only for his own behavior but for that of others and to develop theoretical solutions. The tendency continues to propel him into more predictable behavior in which he becomes future-conscious and less concerned with the here and now. Such concerns tend to make concrete thinking less important, and adults may find him bored and even insulted with their concern for his behavior. If the officer meets such an adolescent, and the adolescent is in difficulty, the boy is probably different from the usual individual who has difficulties with the law. This level of thinking is a mature form of thought process in the normal individual and also represents a higher level of behavior in the deviant individual; however, the skills involved are used for different ends. The ability to hypothesize gives the deviant individual the capacity for adult-level criminal thinking. He may see society as filled with stupid people and opportunities to manipulate and seek selfish ends.

If the officer is faced with such an individual, he may find the confrontation takes the form of special interaction that is unique in police-offender interactions. This individual will be somewhat cool, have a fair knowledge of the law and his rights, and tend to be cooperative and open to the officer's questioning. It may be difficult to tell initially if this kind of reaction and thought process belong to an adolescent who is basically normal and responding to his self-perceived responsibility to cooperate or if the skills are being used to deceive and manipulate. Maturity in thought process is not reserved to law-abiding citizens or adolescents but is also possessed by so-called psychopathic personalities. The psychopathic personality includes as structured a belief system of value as the normal individual has, but the psychopathic personality has a different and atypical belief system. Although most people do not accept criminal behavior and, in fact, feel the responsibility of assuring that all individuals maintain behaviors acceptable to the community, this is one view and not the only way of perceiving the world. Just as individuals from other countries may have different doctrines of political beliefs, many individuals within our culture have other value systems that conflict with those of the general population but may be just as rational to them.

It is natural to feel that individuals who break the law are criminals. Their motivations for breaking the law, however, may be quite different. These range from a desire to obtain material goods to the wish to manipulate others in a very sophisticated way due to a very different belief system. It is difficult to say that such individuals are "sick" or "deviant" except in that they have behaviors that are unacceptable to others. The psychopathic individual often acts out personal motivations that are not unlike those everyone feels at one time or another but is able to repress because of a belief in right and wrong. The psychopathic individual may have developed a different value system through his logical and mature thought process. This makes his crime no less important, but it does suggest a need for understanding such behavior. This individual may be able to deceive and even argue convincingly that what he did was in fact not wrong at all. For these reasons, the officer must be as cautious with the intelligent and mature individual as with the individual who displays inappropriate and immature thought process responses. It must be determined if the adolescent who is very cooperative and mature is an honest and sincere boy or if he is actually a clever and mature psychopathic individual who is attempting to manipulate to prevent his incarceration. The psychopathic individual may take the approach of indicating great remorse for his wrong and throw himself on the mercy of the officer, promising to correct his behavior. The next night he may gleefully commit another burglary.

When faced with a boy who seems honest and capable of mature thinking, the following questions need to be asked to determine if the boy is an individual tending toward psychopathology or is, in fact, a mature adolescent who has simply made a wrong decision or who has become involved unwittingly in an act that was not premeditated:

1. Does the boy live in a home or community that would suggest that his predicament is an unusual circumstance?
2. If the boy is in school, does he have a somewhat clear record, or are there repeated incidents in which his involvement in deviant behavior seems vague?
3. Does he have a record of community activity, good school attendance, and participation?
4. Is he willing to make a long-term commitment that shows his honesty and sincerity?
5. Is he willing to discuss the situation with his parents and the officer?
6. Is the family pattern a normal and community-responsible pattern?
7. Are the parents and the boy willing to assure that such incidents are unusual and that future involvement is unlikely?
8. Does the family indicate willingness to cooperate and to follow up with appropriate controls?
9. Are the boy's usual associates those people who are also involved in appropriate community and school activities?

The preceding points of inquiry are not exhaustive, but they should give the officer a basic direction. The psychopathic boy will often display a history of difficulties, either in school or in the community, although he may never have been involved with the law. His associates will probably be the "outs" of the community, because regardless of how clever he is, his basic psychopathic tendencies will put him at odds with some area of authority. He will often have difficulty making long-term commitments, and his parents either will be resistive or unable to give any assurances of continuing behavioral adjustment. His general family pattern, although it may not be economically deprived, will be one that is in some way atypical. The boy's family may be influential in the community, but there will be distinctive patterns of family behavior that indicate a lack of control by the family or a lack of support in his particular behavioral difficulty. The family may minimize the importance of his behavior or even excuse it as merely a boyish prank.

It is necessary to reemphasize our initial point. At this level of development, the normal adolescent is able to create theories of his own and to hypothesize, which makes it possible to test out behavior through logical thinking rather than acting it out. In this way, the adolescent can actually avoid confrontation through predicting possible outcomes of certain hypothesized behaviors. This skill of creating theories and predicting logical consequences enables the adolescent to behave with increased alternatives and increased responsibility for his behavior.

CREATIVE PROBLEM-SOLVING

With the ability to see relationships and interactive effects of behavior and to hypothesize and make predictions, the adolescent increases his skill in developing solutions to problems. This has the effect of making his behavior more flexible and less frustrating. When he is confronted with a problem, he can reason out how he arrived in such a predicament and can begin to generate a variety of solutions. If this level of thinking were present in all adults, there would be a tremendous decrease in crime. Many chronic criminals are individuals who can neither see nor accept reasons for their behavior. They are individuals who cannot develop creative ways of solving personal problems. Creative problem-solving is very important in the juvenile officer himself, since his role of assisting adolescents often involves providing better solutions than simply arresting a boy. This is why assisting an adolescent in thinking through a problem and arriving at his own alternatives is so important. It forces him toward flexible thinking. The opportunity for this kind of adolescent development is missing in many of our secondary education programs. Many individuals who have marital problems, who cannot deal with their children, or who have constant financial problems are individuals who are unable to develop solutions to their problems. Frequently, child abuse, sexual crimes, and even homicide are the acts of individuals who are immature in adolescent mental development. They simply find themselves in situations for which they see no possible solution except crime or violence.

CLOSURE AND DECENTERING

In any discussion of mental processes, two terms, although somewhat technical, are important to understand. These terms are *closure* and *decentering*. Most people direct their daily activities toward some present or future goal. For some, immediate gratification is necessary, whereas others appear to be very patient in waiting for desired rewards or the realization of some goal. The accomplishment of a goal is referred to as *closure*. Closure occurs at almost every level of human awareness. Drinking water to satisfy a thirst is one example. The satisfaction of personal drives or needs, such as sex drives, needs for material things, wanting to graduate from high school, or obtaining relief from pain, involves closure at a basic level. Closure becomes an act itself. Young children are often impatient and demand immediate gratification, or closure, but with maturity will be willing to delay gratification. This is not always the case, however. As an individual develops higher levels of mental maturity, he is able to delay closure until it is appropriate, through logic and self-understanding. The adolescent usually demonstrates an increasing ability to delay gratification; this ability is an indication of increased maturity.

70

Exceptions do occur, and many adults continue to be somewhat immature in their general personality and thought structure. Television reinforces an immature desire for immediate gratification. Some examples are the instant relief of pain by taking a pill, gaining immediate social acceptance by using a particular deodorant, or the solution in the second half-hour of a murder carried out in the first. Some people suggest that today's young people are not very patient and often want to begin adult life with all of the luxuries that their parents may have struggled a lifetime for. The tendency of the young to want things immediately has also affected sexual morals. In any case, an important sign of increased mental maturity is the willingness or ability to delay closure.

Decentering is another important sign of personal maturity. The word fairly well describes the actual behavior. It is the ability to move one's perception externally and take an objective view of one's own behavior. Like the ability to delay closure, this ability is not always present in adults. This skill is one of great significance to the adolescent and to the adult, since it makes possible unselfish understanding of the needs of others. The adolescent who has not yet reached this level of thought process development will be unable to distinguish between the behavior of others in a given situation and his own subjective involvement. He will be unable to objectively discuss or evaluate what has occurred. He will tend to place blame on someone other than himself. In discussing a situation with such a boy, the officer must take trouble to help the boy review the sequence of events, what his particular role was, and why he holds responsibility for his behavior. This is difficult, but assisting the boy in this clarification process will provide one more experience from which he may slowly begin to adopt the appropriate and mature thinking process that is desired.

IDEALISTIC THINKING

The normal adolescent, developing toward thought process maturation, arrives at a short, wonder-filled phase of mental development called *idealistic thinking*. This level of development may continue into the early phases of adult life if it is achieved in late adolescence. We might call the behaviors associated with this level of thought process development the "life can be a beautiful thing" syndrome. Most people understand this viewpoint and admire it, for everyone would like to believe that life is "a bowl of cherries." The enthusiasm that is generated by adolescents during this phase is contagious, and adults often join the adolescents in their passionate causes and ideals. Idealistic thinking also tends to be the celebration of assuming full responsibility. This is not to say that adult dreamers are not needed, the joyous among us, or that adults cannot be idealists. However, the responsibilities of adult life unfortunately have a tendency to dampen the enthusiasm of idealistic thinking once one begins the daily routine of being a parent and community citizen. Although it is possible to be both joyous and an adult, few, unfortunately, seem to be able to accomplish it.

As wonderful as idealistic thinking is for the adolescent, it can be frustrating for the adults around him and for his friends. This is the time for exposing all that is decadent and for helping to shape a new world. During this phase of mental growth, as we saw in recent years, youths can take to a cause with such fervor that they come in conflict with the law. If such behavior is focused in groups, as we stated earlier, normal adolescents nearing adulthood can become mobs with less than appropriate behavior. Here the law officer finds a force that can reach unbelievable limits. Although it is part of normal adolescent development, this fervent idealism can become a tremendous problem to the juvenile officer. Because such energies originate in well-developed adolescents, the problems created by passionate group movements can be extremely difficult to deal with effectively. These individuals present problems because they attack institutions and aspects of society that even adults admit are not as just as they should be. Difficulties often arise on college campuses because adolescents at a higher level of thought process development are those who reach the level of idealistic thinking.

Fortunately, unknown to the adolescents themselves, such passion is short lived, and the individual proceeds on to the next stage of mental development, which is typified by a more rational thought process. As adolescent idealistic thought gives way to more adult thinking, adolescents realize that the world is not a perfect place. Although one may think of police officers as the villains at certain stages of adolescence, emergence into adulthood gives understanding that crime is not prevented by idealistic thinking but by people who risk their lives to protect others.

MORAL DEVELOPMENT

An important part of thought process development is the changing level of moral development. The young child learns appropriate values from his parents and adheres to them because they bring rewards. That is, when the child is 5 years old, doing the right thing is good because it brings candy, attention, and love. As the child matures into the middle elementary school years, he becomes fascinated with television and Sunday school. Both carry messages that good guys win and bad guys lose. Thus the child displays values that make him think himself good according to the standards of the media and the church. Moral development at this level involves identification with others who are "good boys and girls." Some have referred to this stage of moral development as the "good boy, bad boy" phase: the child perceives morality from the standpoint that it is better to be good than bad, although all the implications of this may not be well understood.

Just before adolescence, children enter a higher stage of moral development in which they become reflective about the law. They become very moralistic and know the intellectual reasons why one should be good. Furthermore, they tend to reject other children who are not good and may even punish them. This is the "cowboy" and "soldier" phase of growing up. It is a time when boys engage in war games in which they fight the forces of evil. The middle-school child becomes very conscious of fair play, and seventh- and eighth-grade teachers find that they must at all cost make their classes fair to all or suffer rejection by the entire class. At this stage, children become quite reactive to adults who are unfair or who do not meet their moral or ethical expectations. The middle-school child is often a moralist, and, if given the opportunity, he would be a far more punitive judge of his peers than any adult.

Whereas the 10- to 14-year-old is a moralist, the adolescent is somewhere between complete confusion and blatant rebellion. In adolescence, the individual is suddenly at odds with all adults and, at the same time, is searching desperately for a code, belief, or value system he can call his own. This is the essence of moral development in adolescence. No longer can adolescents accept childish beliefs of right and wrong; they must test out for themselves the laws that they have previously accepted. They are less in conflict with morals than they are questioning the particular morals that they see around them. They no longer blindly accept the adult concept of morality but must develop their own.

In summary, many adolescent offenders are individuals who are caught in a temporary state of anger and confusion but are basically moral individuals. They are not intentionally confronting the law but, more important, themselves. *Such individuals need as much assistance as possible.* During adolescence, individuals develop what may be called a "personal contract" in regard to moral behavior. They seek basic guidelines for their personal behavior. They are struggling with the final stage of moral development in which they finalize a personal belief system that will take them into adulthood. For most of society, this is the final level of moral development. It is called the "social contract" or "individual rights" level of moral behavior. When this level is completed, sometime in late adolescence or early adulthood, the individual accepts a personal doctrine of behavior and a general ideology of life. Once the adolescent begins to make peace with himself, tremendous changes occur in his behavior, which subsides into more normal and acceptable patterns as he enters adulthood.

ADDITIONAL READINGS

Adams, J. *Understanding adolescence.* Boston: Allyn & Bacon, 1976.

Elkind, D. *Children and adolescence: Interpretive essays on Jean Piaget.* New York: Oxford Press, 1970.

Grinder, R. *Studies in adolescence.* New York: Macmillan, 1975.

Kiell, N. *The universal experience of adolescence.* Boston: International Universities Press and Beacon Press, 1964.

Langer, J. *Theories of development.* New York: Holt, Rinehart & Winston, 1969.

CHAPTER 5

SEXUALITY AND ADOLESCENCE

If I had asked and you had told me,
I still wouldn't listen.

Perhaps no single human act is given more attention in society than sex. It is referred to as an act of love, of passion, of aggression or joy, or of sin or as an experience of honest and open communication. It occupies much of adult society's time but is almost an obsession in adolescence. Sexual behavior is a natural and important aspect of maturing through adolescence. There are few adolescents who do not find the sexual aspect of their being at least temporarily an overwhelming concern at some point in their development. Their concern about sex is not lessened by the frequently poor understanding and experience that adults themselves have of it. Generally, adults' knowledge of sexual function and its consequences is little more developed than that of many adolescents. This lack of knowledge about sex is based, to a large degree, on the social and religious taboos that are so often associated with it; but this does not change the fact that many adults are no more able to deal with issues surrounding sex and sexual behavior than are many adolescents. The juvenile officer may have more experience with sexual problems in adolescence than much of the population; however, a feeling of anxiety is often apparent even when professionals deal with sexual problems involving teenagers.

The issue of sex and associated behaviors is so complex and value laden that it is often difficult to agree on the actual problems involved or on exactly what course of action should be taken to assist adolescents who have special problems in this area. With adequate information, however, the professional officer should be able to apply his knowledge to a particular situation.

SEX AND SEXUALITY

It is helpful to distinguish between what is commonly referred to as "sex" and the more complex issue of "sexuality." In the following discussion, *sex* will imply the act of intercourse or the preliminary to it. When we use the term *sexuality,* we are referring to the more complex behavior that is associated with sexual roles and identity. Whereas adults are more often concerned with the physical act of sex, teenagers are more likely to be concerned about sexuality.

The great issues confronting adolescents involve their basic self-identification as a person and as a sexual being. Despite women's liberation, it is still generally true that boys identify with stereotyped male behaviors and girls with stereotyped female behaviors, as we stated in Chapter 1. Boys are taught to be aggressors, and girls are primarily taught to be passive partners in sexual behaviors. These roles have significant implications for understanding the problems of adolescence. Most boys are concerned with male dominance and aggressive behavior, which are often displayed in the media as attributes of an attractive man. Girls continue to attempt to be pretty, appealing, and seductive to boys. Boys learn early that size of the penis, pubic hair, facial hair, muscles, and other male physical characteristics are important indications of their manliness. These factors play a large role in the early adolescent concerns of boys. The thin boy, the immature boy who develops facial hair late in adolescence, and the boy who appears physically unmanly all suffer, to some degree, from a deflated self-image. Girls learn early that breast size, attractive hair, shapely hips, and various other female physical characteristics will stimulate the interest of boys. Thus, boys and girls who do not display the appropriate attractiveness for their sex often find increased difficulty in developing an adequate self-concept during adolescence. Adolescents who mature late in various sexual characteristics often compensate by adopting nonsexual roles, implying that they do not care if they are "sexy" or not. For the boys, an external or artificial toughness, escape into an academic or intellectual role, avoidance of peers, isolation and involvement with specialized hobbies that preclude sexual contacts, and deviant, aggressive behavior can all be reactions to feelings of sexual unattractiveness. Girls may take the same routes. It is not uncommon to see girls adopt more masculine roles, just as boys may adopt less masculine, effeminate roles.

But what is it all about? Is it so important to be attractive in the first place? Sexual attraction is not merely a prelude to jumping into bed but is a way of verifying one's own developing sexuality. A sexual role and feeling of appropriate sexual identification are an important part not only of self-concept but also of learning how to attract someone of the opposite sex into a loving, mutually accepting relationship. This is the ultimate goal of sexual interaction among adolescents. Boys and girls are looking for a partner from whom they can gain love, security, attention, social acceptance, and sex, with sex falling last on the list. Sex in adolescence is one of the focal points in demonstrating love and affection to another individual. The relationship is the heart of the matter. However, because of the emphasis given to sex by society, the adolescent is often confused and believes that the sex *act* is what it is all about. Adolescents, like adults, cannot spend all of their time in bed; in fact, most of their time is spent out of bed relating to another human being in a positive and loving manner. The passion of love often seen in adolescence and young adulthood is the predecessor of more adult relationships that involve mutual commitment, concern, companionship, and long-term sharing and security. It is sad that many adolescents and a large number of adults never develop this ultimate awareness but continue to act on entirely sexual impulses in their interaction with members of the opposite sex. Pairing relationships in adolescence give the experience and practice that each individual needs to enter a successful adult relationship. Furthermore, temporary relationships in adolescence give the individual an opportunity to develop his own moral beliefs, to test out the teachings of his parents, and to finally adopt a personal belief system. These aspects are much more important than the concern for intercourse on which many adults focus their attention.

MYTHS

It is essential that adults dealing with adolescents remember the pain, confusion, and fear that is associated with relationships and sex when one has no experience except that which is shared by peers or acquired through the media. Understandably, there is a significant amount of unusual adolescent behavior that displays not true personality deviancy but the upsets and anxiety caused by sexual matters. There are many myths and problems associated with adolescence in the area of sex. The juvenile officer should seek out as much literature about sex and sexuality as possible, since the officer is frequently in a better position to assist parents and adolescents in sexual matters than are other adults in the adolescent's world. The following are examples of only some of the many myths associated with sex.

The myth of masturbation as a deviant act

The Romans masturbated and so have most generations since. Few civilizations have crumbled because the young masturbated. However, this normal preadolescent and adolescent behavior has been so shielded from public discussion that many adolescents have severe anxieties and fears about it. One of the most important aspects of masturbation is that, like intercourse, it feels good. Like the young child who touches and rubs his genitals because it feels good, adolescents and adults find the same autoerotic pleasure in more advanced acts of the same nature, regardless of moral and religious taboos. It is not a perverted or deviant act but one that is quite natural. What is not so natural is the tremendous guilt that is often associated with the act because of adult teaching during childhood and adolescence. Certainly, masturbation can become a deviant act, like unhealthy obsessions with food, material items, and so forth. But periodical masturbation is a natural outlet for sexual frustration and tension. One problem is that many adults still carry adolescent guilt associated with masturbation and find themselves unable to deal rationally with an adolescent who has concern about the act.

Girls often have a particular problem in this area because the taboo on masturbation is often taught to them earlier than to boys and is given more emphasis. The deviancy of the act is stressed to the point that actual neurotic feelings may be conditioned into the girl. It is interesting that, until recently, neither boys nor girls realized that many girls masturbate. Many men are surprised to find that girls manage it without a penis. This is further testimony to the lack of knowledge boys usually have about female anatomy. More surprising are girls who don't know they can masturbate.

Masturbation is a basic and early indicator to both boys and girls of their awakening feelings of sexuality. Most individuals become aware of sexual intercourse or associated activity through parents, peers, the media, school social interaction, and learning. Since sexual behavior is closely tied to self-concept relative to becoming an attractive and accepted individual, most adolescents will engage in fantasies or actual masturbation beginning in preadolescence, roughly between the ages of 12 and 14. The reawakening of sex hormone production during preadolescence causes, along with physical changes, emotional changes that foster personal awareness of physical changes related to sexual attractiveness and emotional social interest in the opposite sex.

What effect does this have? First, remember that at this time of life the adolescent is suddenly brought to awareness of issues of personal attractiveness that were not very important during late childhood. The boy or girl in late childhood is not often outer-directed but engages in activities, sports, achievement and, in general, is just one of the family and community. Suddenly, the individual is acutely aware of himself as a person. "Am I too fat? Am I ugly? Do people like me? Am I normal? Will I have friends in high school? How smart am I?" All become critical questions, when only a year ago or months ago such questions were never imagined. This sudden move into the world of sexual relationships and heterosexual interest can be a crisis for any child. For the child who already has a deflated or negative self-concept, it can be the beginning of a frightening period of life. As a consequence, personal exploration and awareness and subtle information-seeking become quiet ways of beginning to "check things out." This first stage of awareness is understandably autoerotic; it may coincide with minor sexual excitement while taking a shower, on seeing a member of the opposite sex, or due to actual masturbation and self-stimulating activity. All of this usually occurs in private moments for the boy or girl and produces great embarrassment and shyness. Since the adolescents are so suddenly aware of themselves, they naturally assume that everyone around them is also aware of their development.

As the adolescent proceeds in relationship development, this brief period of intense self-awareness begins to subside. With careful excursions into interpersonal experimentation, the adolescent moves from personal exploration to interpersonal exploration.

The myth that petting can lead to pregnancy

At the beginning of adolescence, many adolescents have had such limited experience with factual information about sex that myths abound. Girls may be terrified of becoming pregnant but have little real information about exactly how a woman becomes pregnant other than that proximity to a boy is necessary. If the girl doesn't already have enough fears about menstruation, interpersonal contact introduces more, including anxieties about the frequency of or varying periods of time between menstrual periods that are typical when a girl begins to menstruate. Both boys and girls experience heightened anxiety during their first petting experiences. This also adds to the confusion and general anxiety that both may have about interaction.

In some individuals, fear and anxiety about sex may become so acute that severe emotional problems result, causing isolation, aggression, suicide, and other deviant reactions. This is why adolescents who come into contact with juvenile authorities may often be individuals whose behavior is, in some manner, associated with sexual behavior.

The myth that people who don't like members of the opposite sex are "gay"

At the same time that adolescents experience such concern about their personal identity and sexuality, they also become aware of sexually different individuals, that is, homosexuals. Much adolescent concern about homosexuality and frequently severe reactions to it are based in adolescents' deep personal fears about their own sexual capabilities. Because of their fear of sexual inability, they may react strongly to anyone who demonstrates what they feel is sexual incompetency. This is often particularly true in lower socioeconomic groups where sexual aggressiveness and manhood may be more important than in upper socioeconomic groups. There seems to be a general relationship between an individual's level of education and his acceptance of homosexuality. This suggests that boys from families in which male stereotypes are influential are likely to have the most negative reaction to homosexuality as well as the most severe personal reactions to fears of sexual inability. This is why aggressive and extremely punitive adult treatment of such adolescent boys provokes such antiauthority reactions. The boy may be overcompensating for a poor sexual image by being more aggressive and daring to prove his manhood, of which he is quite uncertain.

Thus, it is extremely important to recognize that homosexuality and the myths surrounding it may be a concern of many adolescents. If the adolescent is already having difficulty with his self-concept and his sexual identity, the tremendous social and religious persecution of "gay" people tends to greatly intensify this anxiety in boys and often in girls.

The adolescent's personal concern about homosexuality is somewhat prevalent until the individual begins to have successful heterosexual relationships. When dealing with adolescents who have some sort of personal problem, the juvenile officer should be sensitive to this anxiety and recognize its importance.

Some brief comments should be made concerning the entire issue of homosexuality and the gay liberation movement. The following statements may be useful in the further exploration of this area as an alternative to the more traditional role of legal rejection of all homosexual acts and relationships.

1. Homosexuality has been an aspect of all cultures in history and does not always imply "sickness" or perversion.
2. Common reasons for the negative reaction to homosexuality by the average individual are religious training and personal insecurity about one's own sexual identity. The personality of the gay individual may be no less or more peculiar than that of most people.
3. There are "sick" and normal gay people as there are "sick" and normal heterosexuals. The fact that many people find homosexual behavior repulsive does not mean that it is a disturbed behavior. In fact, the American Psychiatric Association no longer includes homosexuality as a classification of personality disorder.
4. Homosexuality remains, however, a personal life style rejected by most of society.
5. Adolescents who demonstrate homosexual tendencies or who openly identify with the "gay" movement should obtain counseling by social behavioral professionals to assist them in personal adjustment in a culture that is unaccepting of them.
6. Given the current legal restrictions on homosexual behavior and indecent liberties, which the officer is obliged to enforce, the attitude toward homosexual behavior should be as objective as possible in any attempt to morally judge and react to such individuals.
7. All juvenile officers will need assistance and additional training in the area of homosexuality, and this training should be provided through departmental programs where the issues can be discussed and departmental policies developed. Homosexuality will continue to be a significant area of controversy during the coming years.

It is important for the juvenile officer to recognize that many adolescents display personal identity problems in the sexual area, one of which may be the fear of being homosexual. This fear is often associated with the need to become an acceptable boy or girl; underlying anxiety may stimulate deviant behavior that could result in conflict with law officials. Adolescents, in their quest to become adults, may temporarily display

81

deviant behavior due to sexual identity problems or fears and phobias about sex.

The myth that venereal disease can be contracted by touching

Because of a lack of factual information, many adolescents go to creative extremes to avoid venereal disease, whereas others appear totally ignorant of the existence of the diseases. Some of these adolescents probably believe that it couldn't happen to them. This belief is an indictment of the parents and schools that apparently supply too little information; the increase of venereal diseases in recent years is challenged only by the record number of G.I. cases during World War II. Oddly, it seems that much of the population is not concerned about or even aware of the problem. One reason for this apathetic attitude on the part of adults and teenagers is the almost childlike belief in today's medical cure-alls. Many "kids" go to the family doctor and discover they have some form of venereal disease, which they casually assume some form of medication will immediately "cure." Ignorance about the way venereal disease is transmitted is only one of the problems surrounding it. The consequence of the lack of information and the casual attitude is an alarming increase in venereal disease among teenagers. Again, the juvenile officer may be in a position to become involved with the problem at a more critical level than others. Professional training is needed in this area but is often not a priority in local police departments.

These four myths concerning venereal disease, homosexuality, pregnancy, and masturbation are only examples of the many problems adolescents encounter because of a lack of adequate information. The entire area of sexual development and sexual behavior is one in which juvenile officers need much additional training, since they are often in a position to deal with the effects of sexual difficulties. In a sense, the juvenile officer is the last chance for intervention in both personality and social disorders related to adolescent sexual development.

SEXUAL ROLE IDENTITY

As the adolescent begins to mature, he has to reconcile his own personality with his sexual role. This, of course, is also true of girls. The sexual role stereotypes are culturally well defined, and individuals who can adapt to these stereotypes may find less difficulty in eventual role identification. However, in recent years both boys and girls have been encouraged to adopt newer role identities that break somewhat with the traditional sexual roles. For example, boys have tended to become less dominant and aggressive, their clothing styles reflect a more effeminate model, and dating practices have altered to allow boys to be more submissive. Girls have tended to become more aggressive and independent, to wear more masculine and functional clothing, and to expect more freedom in their activities. Adults have also reflected this general trend. There are now many young adults who have matured, married, and entered the community with life styles greatly different from their parents'. Many young couples are less likely to begin a family than in past years and often both continue to work after marriage. Living together without legal marriage has become much more common. More choices exist for both sexes in adopting sexual role models, and this may have lessened the crisis of sexual role identity for the adolescent in past years.

The behaviors that boys and girls can now display in adolescence, although liberalized, have caused many problems for the adolescents themselves and for adults who find their behavior alien. For example, girls who attempt to be more assertive and gain "ranging" privileges, such as boys traditionally have, often become involved in serious arguments and difficulties with both male and female parents. The fathers, still somewhat traditional in beliefs about how young girls should act, and the mothers, who often see the aggressive behavior of their daughters as unfeminine and even promiscuous, may create an atmosphere of family interaction so heated that the young girl becomes confused and angry enough to run away. In recent years, runaway girls have become a national crisis, causing tremendous pain and anxiety to parents. The general public seems to think that the problem only involves lower-class or undesirable adolescents. In fact, girls run away from upper-class and educated families, from middle-class, lower-class, farm, factory, and professional families. It cannot be claimed that changing sexual roles for girls created the tremendous runaway problem, but this cultural change is a contributing factor.

Perhaps no other recent sexual role change has created a greater problem for both adolescents and adults than long hairstyles for boys. This problem is lessening now, and the public appears well on its way to forgetting the intensity of feeling, the lawsuits against schools, and the tremendously negative identity given to boys with long hair by adults at the beginning of the fashion trend. Long hair, however, was one indication that a major rebellion against not only authority but traditional sexual roles was in progress. Whereas the wearing of long hair was a dramatic and important symbol of a temporary challenge by youths to the adults in society, the accompanying issues included changing beliefs about sexual roles. More than telling adults not to interefere and to let them be themselves, adolescents were searching for a new role as individuals. That search included a confused attempt to avoid the stereotype of the "all-American male." Drug abuse, violent and law-challenging behaviors, and increasing gang orientation of many youths in recent years have often obscured the more profound implications of the sexual

83

change that was in progress. One of the major changes involved an attempt to develop a more flexible model of sexual behavior for both boys and girls. This included more equalized roles, more interpersonal sensitivity and honesty, and increased sharing of being human without traditional feminine and masculine role play. It was a grand rebellion, but it failed.

There are many indications that boys and girls today tend to adopt more traditional sexual identities. In clinical work with adolescents in trouble, there now appears an adolescent need for more stability, conformity, and a return to traditional roles. Adolescents appear to be searching for a stable model that they can accept and integrate with their own personal identity. These roles are becoming more similar to the traditional roles that most adults understand and have used in their own development toward adulthood. This trend, praised by more traditional adults and law officials, is important for a very basic reason: the adolescent who continues to rebel, to attempt to be "different," and to confront authority will more probably be an adolescent with significant problems than a normal adolescent who is joining "the movement."

In elementary schools, high schools, and colleges across the country, there is an obvious and dramatic change in the typical adolescent. Both boys and girls are looking for stability and security, for places to "fit in," and they are more serious about preparing for a job and taking a place in the "straight" community. This trend will probably continue, and in many ways the loss of the enthusiasm and energy generated by youths in recent years is unfortunate. There have been some noticeable results, however, of the recent revolt against tradition.

One result is that the adolescent of today appears to have somewhat more humanistic values than either adolescents or adults had in the past. The adolescent today is more likely to question the validity of a law or value in a current context than to judge it by its religious and social acceptability. This attitude is not rebellious but reflects a higher level of moral development. Adolescents who question values and laws rationally are usually more mature than many adults. Law officers need to be careful not to mistake the argument and logic of today's adolescent for deviant or rebellious behavior. This is why talking to teenagers to attempt to determine the reason for their confrontation with the law is important. If the adolescent is deviant and rebellious, then there will be dogmatic and unreasonable resistance. If the adolescent is a thinking, "straight" individual, he should be allowed to express his belief, although he may have to obey a law questionable to him and to the officer as well.

A second result of the revolt against tradition is that the adolescent boy or girl today may not fit the sexual stereotype but still be regarded as an adjusted and normal teenager. Behavioral stereotypes still exist and are even more similar to those of the past. However, many adolescents are living out somewhat altered roles. We probably will have to accept these modifications of traditional sexual roles and recognize that the associated behaviors are as appropriate as those usually expected. For example, many girls now are assertive and independent compared with most girls several years ago. Often, when a male adult is faced with such an adolescent girl, he is "turned off" and becomes hostile. Rather than the girl's being in any way truly deviant, it is more likely that the man feels that his own sexual identity and dominance are being challenged. Conversely, many boys today are allowed and even encouraged to be more effeminate than their fathers or older brothers were. Effeminate behavior, mannerisms, or interests are no longer seen as "queer," or homosexual, by other adolescents. This acceptance of a broader range of male behaviors, from aggressive to effeminate and nonaggressive, has tended to make homosexual, or gay, behavior less important. Many adolescents have both heterosexual and gay friends, although they are themselves decidedly heterosexual, because the past rebellion has produced youths who are more accepting of a wide range of sexual roles in both boys and girls. This has tremendous implications for the juvenile officer. It means that more attention must be focused on the individual and less on his or her sexual role behavoir. If the officer reacts to sexual behavior other than that in conflict with the law, then the problems of law enforcement may be increased in complexity. More attention must be focused on the law itself and less on stereotyped expectations that often, unfortunately, become part of the enforcement function. How the officer feels about masculine girls or effeminate boys should be dealt with at the personal level and not in situations with adolescents who have confronted the law. This is not easy.

There are exceptions to the adolescent behavior under discussion, of course. An officer may say, "All that may be true for some kids, but most of the kids I see never heard about it." This is a valid reaction. There are farming communities, big city ghettos, small villages, and other types of communities where the rebellion over hairstyles, sexual roles, or dating practices has not produced change in recent years. If anything, these communities have become more traditional. For example, in many groups there continues to be a fierce dedication to the male stereotype of toughness, aggression, and dominance. Homosexual individuals are still seen as "fags" and deserving of disdain. Girls are expected to function according to male needs that are pretty well defined. In most cases, the girls accept this role. Although in these groups business goes on as usual, it is important to recognize that, in other communities and in much of the country, things have changed.

Nothing changes a social group as much as affluence and education.

One reason that recent social sexual role changes have not affected many groups may be that those groups have not shared in the growing affluency and educational opportunities of other groups. In groups from lower social strata and with poor educational backgrounds, it is likely that traditional sexual stereotypes will exist, often out of necessity. Language and knowledge contribute to change in the individual, giving him more awareness and the opportunity to adopt his own way of life. If an individual cannot talk his way out of a situation, he may have to fight his way out. If aggression is a determining factor in behavior, then boys most frequently will take the lead. With less language capacity and knowledge, an individual is left to fight for what is his in the best way he can. Poverty and ignorance force an individual into primitive ways of living and acting; the primitive code states that the man goes out and fights for survival while the woman takes care of the home and children. In such a situation one does not have the need or the opportunity to worry about sexual roles, because they are already firmly established and are demanding. Consequently, any individual who holds other values is not to be trusted. This includes individuals who adopt unusual sexual roles or life styles, which are not only incomprehensible but threatening to whatever little identity the others have established. It should be remembered, however, that such individuals, men or women, would probably change their roles if given the opportunity to do so. Community action programs, job training services, day care centers, and equal opportunity in education all serve to give the struggling individual an opportunity to join the mainstream of society. For the present, however, social and sexual roles in some segments of society have not changed or been affected by the same factors that affect the larger society. This also makes it important that the juvenile officer gain training in sexual role problems, since they will affect his or her interaction with adolescents from all parts of society.

The importance of sexual role identity is its significance in establishing a personal identity. An adult can, through years of maturation and experience, begin to establish a personal identity that does not depend so heavily on sexuality. There are also adolescents who do not depend on their sexuality as a basis for personal identification, but these youths are unusual. For most adolescents, sexuality plays a significant role in establishing a personal identity. It is simply very difficult to avoid or deny sexuality during a stage of life when dramatic physical and emotional changes are taking place.

The most critical consequence of establishing one's sexual role identity is the development of an acceptable personal identity. Sexual role identity is one of the factors that leads to a personal identity; it is combined with factors such as socioeconomic identity, intellectual identity, athletic and general physical competency, and social group identity to provide the basis for the individual's development of a total personal identity. Personal identity is that inner feeling of selfhood, or personal integration, and self-awareness that affects how an individual reacts to the environment and how he directs his behavior and interests. Following is a detailed discussion of personal identity from which the juvenile officer may gain an understanding of how this factor both causes behavior and acts as an inhibitor of behavior in varying situations.

PERSONAL IDENTITY

The establishment of a personal identity is a fluid and dynamic process of personal awareness. No one is able to develop and maintain a static personal identity over long periods of time unless he is disturbed or severely incompetent. Such individuals exist. In adolescence, the individual is in the process of establishing a personal identity that will provide the basis for adult behavior. In adulthood, the individual will continue to alter his personal identity, but in adolescence the first major attempt is made to establish himself as a distinct individual, separate from his parents. This period of maturation is very important and can certainly be expected to involve much energy and conflict as the individual breaks with his childhood identification with the personalities of family and friends and establishes a separate and distinct personality. As we stated in the discussion of sexual role identity, there are several factors that contribute to this developing personal concept.

Sexual role identity is a major personal and social factor in determining self-concept, or personal identity. If a boy feels that he is an attractive male and is content with that identity, then he probably will have positive feelings about his acceptability to other boys, to girls, and to parents and teachers. He will also feel like a member of a group; this should provide security and stability in his interaction with others. Since he feels good about himself, he will be more cooperative and accepting of others, although they may be less attractive or typical. Reinforcement from the social group also may stimulate interest in achievement and in participating in school and community organizations and activities. If the boy has average or better intellectual development, then he probably does well in school. Furthermore, he will probably set life or occupational goals that are acceptable to family and friends. In this case, several interacting factors produce a general personal concept that is positive and appropriate to social expectations.

This sort of adaptive behavior is an ideal outcome in development. Many youths have difficulty in some area of developing a personal identity, and this difficulty alters, to some degree, their personal identity. How much his identity is altered from the norm of the youth's social group will correspond to possible personal difficulties. Not all individuals who have difficulty end up in court or the juvenile center; conversely, most adolescents who have poorly developed identities adopt successful behaviors in order to avoid problems at school or in the community. The key to understanding these adolescents is to understand deviant adaptation.

Adaptive behavior is important for survival in a hurried and often chaotic world. Without adaptive ability, few would last out the year. However, not all individuals are able to alter their behavior in different situations or stay flexible enough to meet new situations successfully with different behaviors. If an individual is suddenly forced into a wheelchair because of illness, many behaviors will have to be changed if he is to successfully adapt to his new life style. If he cannot adapt, then he will become disturbed or severely depressed until he is able to adapt.

Some individuals adapt their behavior in ways that are not acceptable to others or are harmful to the individual. This is called *deviant adaptation*. An individual can refuse to adapt at all and find himself in an ever-worsening situation, or he may adopt a deviant behavioral alternate. Criminality is often based on the individual's deviant attempt to adapt to the environment. For example, the boy who does poorly in school and who is not well accepted by typical adolescents still has to develop a personal identity, like any other adolescent. However, if this boy accepts the feedback from his world, he will develop a defeated and negative self-concept that will be personally destructive. The human tendency is to be adaptive and to avoid, at all costs, accepting feedback from others that damages the self-concept. If possible, an individual will try to alter his behavior to be more acceptable if he finds that others do not like him. But suppose the problem is school achievement and he has never done well in school. Suppose that elementary school teachers passed him each year because he appeared too stupid to learn by repeating. In high school, he finds that one has to make at least passing grades to be accepted. However, because of his poor learning in elementary school, he is unable to successfully learn although he wants to, because he simply does not have the skills. He cannot change or adapt his behavior, because the tools simply are not there, nor is there time to develop them. However, he will not believe that he is stupid or less valuable as a person than those who do well in school. What can he do when he must develop some sort of positive belief about himself? He develops a deviant adaptation. He rejects school and all teachers as being unfair. He develops the belief that those kids who have money always get the most attention, and he sets into motion a personal rebellion against the rich, the politicians, the teachers, and other individuals, including police. He can develop a Robin Hood self-concept that will provide a stable, heroic, and effective personal identity and provide goals.

From our example, it can be seen that in cases where a boy or girl cannot adopt a positive personal identity through normal identification processes, adaptive behavior can provide an effective although deviant identity. In this way poor children, ugly children, and those with poor physical abilities, low intellectual abilities, or other problems may be forced into deviant personal identities and become delinquent. Not all children who have deficiencies develop deviant adaptive behavior. However, it is probable that most children who encounter significant problems in adolescence are having difficulty in developing a positive personal identity.

Once a personal identity is established, entire clusters of behaviors are learned as a consequence. How the adolescent sees himself determines what interests he will have, and these interests will require that he engage in and practice certain behaviors to the exclusion of others. With increased specialization in experiences, he will eventually develop definite personal role expectations. If the adapted behaviors involve criminal activity, then he will learn his profession and develop a personal identity that will be extremely difficult, if not impossible, to alter. This is why the juvenile officer needs to understand the importance of forming a positive personal identity during adolescence.

The juvenile officer should understand that chronic behavioral problems in an adolescent are not the result of his being a "bad kid" but of his environment and of a situation that prevents his being normal. This may seem a sad state of affairs, but the adolescent who takes this direction is also displaying vital and energized capabilities for personal change. If he can be reached early and given assistance in developing a positive personal identity, the problem of chronic delinquency can be avoided. However, such intervention requires far more than simply confronting the youth with the law.

The juvenile officer must realize why youths who have made deviant adaptations in personal identity development must resist in confrontations with the law. From our discussion, it should be understood that deviant adaptation is a personality adaptation made to establish personal identity. If the adolescent gives in to the law and accepts the implication that he is "bad" or incompetent, then his entire self-concept is destroyed. The survival of an intact personality is at stake. Related to manifest deviant behavior are various personal self-concept structures involving sexual role identification, economic identification, and social group identification. The only way to resolve these complex problems through legal intervention is with long-term and isolated treatment in an institutional setting. However, if the adolescent is in the process of making a deviant adaptation, there is still time to intervene at the level of his own community before his personal identity becomes so hardened that the more drastic approach must be taken.

INTERPERSONAL BEHAVIOR

At the heart of sexuality is the recognition of one's own sexual role and personal identity. As sexual role and personal identity are established, the individual proceeds into the middle to late adolescent phase, where he begins to look toward a relationship with a member of the opposite sex. The development of such a relationship is critical, since he will need the verification and exchange of affection of an interpersonal relationship to completely establish his sexuality. During this phase, the adolescent yearns for a partner, for another individual who can share his dreams, his concerns, and his plans. This is the beginning of the "pairing" phase of adolescence; the individual begins in earnest to practice relationships that will result in a family adult role.

During the early stages of adolescence, the individual often is involved in group identification as a means of establishing personal identity and of resolving the discontinuity crisis. As these issues are resolved, his attention will be focused more on individual relationships and less on group membership. This is true for both boys and girls. As the individual moves into late adolescence, he becomes concerned with the establishment of a relationship in which some stability in his personal life can be achieved. This need is a natural consequence of both the resolution of personal discontinuity and a growing feeling of personal autonomy and independence. The battles with parents and family over growing independence have subsided, and the adolescent is allowed much more freedom as others begin to accept him as a young adult who is able to take responsibility for himself. This period of development is roughly between the ages of 17 and 19, at the time many adolescents are entering their senior year of high school. Compared with early and middle adolescence, this is a much more stable and happy period. Often the adolescent has a part-time job and a first car, or at least freer use of the family car. He has status as one of the oldest members of the school community. Graduation from high school is now impending as are postgraduation plans and goals. However, the adolescent is still relatively free from responsibilities and able to engage in social and special interest activities somewhat unencumbered. It is a good time of life.

In this new and exciting phase of adolescent maturity, the individual begins to look for someone with whom to share time and to explore possibilities of more permanent relationships. Individuals who only recently were members of heterosexual "gangs" or groups now begin to drift into pairing relationships. Less time is spent in large groups and more in heterosexual pairs. Practice for permanent relationships now become serious, and the "old gang" begins to break up. This last stage of development has its own trials and tribulations. If group acceptance and recognition caused many periods of anxiety in early adolescence, problems associated with pairing relationships provide at least as much anxiety, mixed with excitement of the highest order. This period of trial relationships has a dramatic effect on the personal behavior of the individual. On the positive side, personal responsibility in a relationship provokes an almost dramatic change in the behavior of many adolescents who only months before were fighting with their parents, arguing with teachers, and seeming to seek every opportunity to confront and test the limits of authority. Suddenly, as a consequence of forming a pairing relationship, the individual becomes more conscious of personal responsibility to others. Even parents again become worthwhile individuals from whom to seek advice, and teachers often note with pleasure an increased interest in school and in preparing for postgraduation work or training. The adolescent now begins to take his interpersonal relationship quite seriously and often asks many questions about what mom and dad did when they were teenagers or exactly how one goes about being a good partner in a relationship. This comes not only as a welcome surprise to adults but often creates a renewed harmony; when the adolescent leaves forever, the parents are wishing that it would not end after all.

However, there are some very serious moments for the adolescent as he experiences the prfound consequences of a relationship. One of the difficulties is in the area of sex and personal interaction. Today many adolescents enter this period with much more sexual knowledge and experience than their parents had. Liberalism and recent changes in sexual role expectations have made it possible for both boys and girls to have sexual relationships without the traditional hang-ups that created anxiety and guilt in the past. This new liberalism appears to be related to another major factor—the Pill. Many teenagers use birth control pills; there is also a variety of other means of birth control available that give the girl much of the responsibility that, only a few years ago, belonged to boys. In the past, the girl was often inhibited by the real possibility of becoming pregnant. The boy not only often felt less guilt about sexual relationships than did girls, but society actually encouraged and expected him to have relations. The girl was expected to worry about birth control, and often it was felt to be her fault if pregnancy did occur. Now girls are relatively free of this concern and tend to take a more active role in sexual matters. There is little doubt that there is more sexual activity among teenagers than there was a few years ago. However, all of the basic fears and anxieties about "how to do it" and consequences of sexual involvement and the various personal fears about being intimate that all have felt at one time or another still occur. Instead of moralizing about sexual relationships before marriage, adults would be far more effective if they discussed frankly the meaning and consequences of sexual relationships.

91

In many ways, the new sexual freedom has created a tremendous problem for adolescents of which they are not even aware. So much emphasis has been given to sex and sexual liberalization in the media that many adolescents find that the physical aspect of the relationship is the actual basis of the relationship. That is, they assume that the substance of a loving relationship is the actual physical encounter. Without it, many individuals feel they do not have a relationship. Less intimate sharing of feelings and concerns and less commitment to continue the relationship if things do not work out well seem to be common. The couple feels that they are in love when it may be merely a temporary attraction.

Interestingly enough, the liberalized sexual roles tend to reinforce the old stereotypes. The basic reason for the relationship is very often sexual compatibility, and physical sex in itself is often a very male-female act characterized by stereotyped behavior. This physical focus tends to make the couple less aware of the other qualities of a relationship.

SUMMARY

How well the individual adolescent progresses through these stages of development determines how enduring his adult adjustment will be. The juvenile officer must understand not only the temporary phases of adolescent development that may be related to sexuality and sex but also the possible deviations that provoke behaviors in conflict with the law. The preceding discussion gives the juvenile officer more information with which to understand the problems of the adolescent. The officer should be encouraged to read more detailed information, and departmental officials should be asked to include seminars on sex and sexuality in in-service training sessions.

ADDITIONAL READINGS

Cohn, F. *Understanding sexuality.* Englewood Cliffs, N.J.: Prentice-Hall, 1974.

Friedman, R. & Richart, R. *Sex differences in behavior.* New York: John Wiley & Sons, 1974.

Goldstein, B. *Human sexuality.* New York: McGraw-Hill, 1976.

Hettlinger, R. *Human sexuality: A psychosocial perspective.* Belmont, Calif.: Wadsworth, 1974.

Maccoby, E., & Jacklin, C. *The psychology of sex difference.* Stanford, Calif.: Stanford Press, 1974.

Wilson, S., Roe, R., & Autrey, L. *Readings in human sexuality.* New York: West, 1975.

CHAPTER 6

THE ADOLESCENT AND PHYSIOLOGICAL-EMOTIONAL DISORDERS

I woke up in the night and knew that I was no longer a child,
That you were no longer responsible.

Juvenile delinquency is a difficult phenomenon to accurately describe and even more difficult to define within limits that are acceptable to a wide range of juvenile authorities. *Juvenile delinquency* as defined by the International Association of Police Chiefs refers to antisocial behavior of young people. Many acts that are not criminal if committed by adults are classified as delinquent transgressions when committed by children. In a broad sense, juvenile delinquency refers to antisocial acts of children and of young people under a given age or "all those thoughts, actions, desires, and strivings which deviate from moral and ethical principles."[1]

In this book we are not attempting to define juvenile delinquency but are suggesting that the response to causal factors may be deviant but return to normal developmental foundations of adolescent growth. In this chapter we will survey briefly some factors that may affect normal adolescent growth and development and that can, under certain circumstances, propel the youth into deviant behavior.

FACTORS UNDERLYING NORMAL ADOLESCENT GROWTH

Physiological growth can affect the behavior of the adolescent temporarily or over a long period of time. The problems we will discuss are physiological rather than social or psychological, but the reader should understand that these factors cannot be easily separated from the behavior of the adolescent. There are at least five major areas of physiological growth and development that interact to produce an adolescent's adaptive behavior:

1. *Perceptual-motor development* involves the adolescent's capabilities in general coordination, balance, fine motor skills, visual abilities, and neurological ability to process sensory information.
2. *Language development* involves the acquisition of language, speech production, communication, and basic capabilities in assimilating verbal information and knowledge. This area also involves memory ability and skill in problem-solving.
3. *Social and personality skills* involve the child's general temperament, character, social adjustment, value structure, and general mental health or social adaptability.
4. *School achievement and adjustment* involve basic learning skills and acquisition of appropriate attitudes and skills for competent academic performance.
5. *Physiological and psychoneurological maturity* involves basic hormonal, metabolic, neurological, nutritional, and other physical changes.

These five areas of growth and development are interactive. There is little doubt that children who exhibit difficulties in any one of these areas will also have problems in others. As the child matures into an adolescent, changes in these areas interact in various ways to cause periods of stress and difficulties in general behavioral adjustment. For example, the adolescent who matures physically late in adolescence may display social or emotional responses to his or her lack of appropriate physical growth that can dramatically affect behavior briefly or over an extended period of time. Children with perceptual difficulties often have problems in learning that lead to poor social or emotional adjustment in school. An atypical social or family environment can affect not only the child's school adjustment but also his or her choice of diets or health care.

Although the police officer cannot hope to be well versed in all of these areas of development, it is important for him to be aware of the multiple factors that contribute to adolescent behavior. This is why so many professionals have difficulty in agreeing on a precise definition of delinquency. Even the experts have difficulty gathering and understanding all of the information available on causes of behavioral delinquency. It is also important to recognize that the adolescent, going through a particularly difficult and fluctuating period of development, is no less prone to behavioral manifestations of developmental difficulty than the many adults who are incarcerated by courts across the country. Poor nutrition, physical disorders, and diseases can cause behavioral difficulties in both adolescents and adults. The adolescent with a physical disorder presents a particularly difficult problem in that he is in a transitional period in which physical change is inherent, that is, adolescence. The adult with specific behavioral changes due to physical disorders or disease can more easily be recognized.

In the following discussion, we want to highlight several developmental factors in adolescent deviant behavior that go beyond the usual social or emotional factors discussed elsewhere. Although adolescents may display behavioral difficulties due to psychological or emotional factors, there are a number of more subtle factors that can also play a dramatic role. Unfortunately, the police officer seldom has the time or the medical resources to check for some of the difficulties cited here. If every adolescent could be screened through a complete physical examination before an incarceration, a significant number would display some definite medical disorder that contributes to their delinquency. Frequently, medical treatment might be substituted for incarceration if the deviant behavior, although related to social and personality factors, were based to a significant degree on physical problems. For the same reason, medical evaluation should be available during retention of the adolescent, if incarceration is indicated. However, as we stated before, too often the police officer, although he may suspect a physical basis for the adolescent's behavior, has few if any resources available to help him accurately assess the actual physiological status of the individual. If the officer has an awareness that health problems cause behavioral problems, then he may be able to encourage investigation of these factors by the courts. This chapter is intended to give the officer some general information concerning medical aspects of adolescent behavior. More detailed readings are listed at the end of the chapter for the officer who wishes to explore this area further.

PHYSICAL DISORDERS THAT AFFECT BEHAVIOR
Epilepsy

Epilepsy has long been regarded by much of the population as a terrible disease in which the person is prone to "fits" and convulsions. Most people not only misunderstand epilepsy but regard individuals with the disorder as dangerous or sick. They will avoid contact if possible for fear that those associated with the individual may contract the disease. The most common form of epilepsy involves *grand mal* seizures. *Petit mal* seizures are less spectacular and may even go unnoticed by those observing the individual. In both cases the individual becomes temporarily unconscious, either for a few seconds or for a longer period, after which he appears to recover fully. The causal factors in epilepsy vary but usually involve brain damage or dysfunction. Most frequently, the condition is controlled by medication. Grand mal seizures require appropriate responses from available adults that are often taught in basic occupational training of police officers.

There are other forms of seizure behavior that may or may not be referred to as epilepsy, although the causal factors are similar. For example, the form of seizure associated with *temporal lobe epilepsy* does not correspond to the classic grand mal behaviors. In this form of epilepsy, because of the area of the brain affected, the individual does not have convulsions or display petit mal seizure behavior. The seizure does not cause any apparent loss of consciousness, and the individual may continue to move or act out behaviors initiated before the seizure. Cases have been recorded in which an individual has completed rather complex acts without awareness at the time or any memory of those acts after the seizure. The individual behaves in a somewhat automated manner and may perform rather bizarre acts. These seizures may be preceded by anxiety and agitation. Some individuals, because of their own reaction and the reaction of others to their problem, exhibit aggressiveness in general behavior. There is often an accompanying emotional component in the behavior of individuals known to have epilepsy, regardless of its form. This behavior is stimulated by the emotional reaction to having a disorder and not from the disorder itself.

There are some forms of seizure behavior that are set off by flashing lights, by music, and even by engaging in prolonged reading. The nature and treatment of epilepsy are complex, and adults involved with the epileptic child or adolescent should understand, as well as possible, the characteristics of the disorder.

The police officer on the street obviously will not be able to attribute an adolescent's behavior to epilepsy through some sort of "street" diagnosis. For example, the behavior of an individual with a temporal lobe seizure could closely resemble the behavior of someone taking drugs. In cases where there is bizarre behavior or where an individual appears dazed or unaware while still mobile, the police officer should take the adolescent to a safe area for observation and request medical assistance. Careful notes on the individual's behavior should be taken, and he should have a brief medical examination at some point during detention. If an adolescent is to be retained for some time, then a medical and family history taken by court or detention personnel should be included as a routine part of the procedure.

Tumors, brain damage, and drug-induced disorders

There is a wide range of behaviors that can result from various neurological difficulties. During the stormy changes in the adolescent physiological system, latent neurological difficulties may be manifested in extreme behavior, ranging from unusually docile behaviors to episodes of unprovoked rage, hostility, and aggression. Various specific forms of brain damage, temporary neurological disorders, or drug-induced cerebral dysfunction can cause temporary periods of deviant behavior, lasting for a few hours up to several months or even years. In the case of tumors or lesions in some area of the brain, there may be dramatic changes in an individual's behavior that cannot be explained solely on the basis of adolescent maturation. Police officers are always alert to the homicidal individual; however, in each case of overt homicidal behavior, careful medical examination and medical history-taking should be performed before assuming that the individual is simply reacting to a poor home or community environment. The nervous system is tremendously complex; even today much less is known about its function than most people would assume. The most effective method of recognizing neurological problems is a case history taken by a capable social worker who is alerted by the complete behavioral observations made by the police officer. If there is some suspicion of unusual behavior, then a complete medical examination should be requested as part of the court workup. It is difficult to determine how many individuals who come in contact with the law have some minimal brain dysfunction contributing to their total behavior.

97

The recent problem with drugs is well known to most police officers. Results of studies concerning the effects of marijuana on the nervous system are conflicting and confusing. Certainly, "hard" drugs have been a continuing problem. Their effects include addiction, physical deterioration, and severe mental disorders. However, the effects of drugs such as alcohol and marijuana are more controversial and more variable, ranging from brain damage to sexual dysfunction. Continued use of any drug can change an individual's behavior significantly. Our own experience with individuals using alcohol and marijuana suggests that continual and habitual use does impair perceptual and conceptual functioning, with the probability of significant impairment of the neurological system. Individuals who have been habitual users of drugs should always be given a complete medical examination if they are to be incarcerated.

Some characteristics that should suggest the need for a medical or neurological examination are:

1. Bizarre behaviors that, based on a family history, are generally uncharacteristic of the adolescent and are displayed over a relatively brief period of time.
2. Unprovoked behavior, on confrontation, that is unrealistic or inappropriate for a normal individual and that may be dangerous to the individual or others.
3. Automated behavior in which the individual seems "foggy," partially conscious, or in a stupor that cannot be attributed to drug or alcohol usage.
4. Blind, or undifferentiated, rage and aggression in which the individual appears to be striking out with no definite target or goal.
5. Inability to articulate, or speak clearly, without any significant indication of drug usage.
6. Minor flickering of the eyelids, stiffening of the body without total loss of control, apparent lack of comprehension of what others are saying, or unstable movements.
7. Temporary loss of memory and directional or time orientation, possibly accompanied by confusion and fear about where the individual is at the time.
8. General confusion, apparent inability to respond to questions, overwhelming periods of fatigue, and intermittent periods of euphoria or happiness.
9. Extremely hyperactive behavior, restlessness, or inability to relax or to control himself.
10. Bizarre fears or unfounded anxiety, or both.

Language-related brain damage

Language is the means by which an individual is able to gather information, organize thoughts, recall information, and communicate with others. Language is more than words and is certainly more than speech. Children who have difficulty in learning sometimes are also individuals who have a syndrome that has recently been described as *minimal brain dysfunction.* This is a general term used primarily in education and psychology to imply that an individual has some minimal brain damage or dysfunction that, although possibly affecting specific areas of behavior, does not incapacitate the individual, as does retardation, for example. One area in which minimal brain dysfunction can be evident is that of learning and using language.

A major difference between minimal dysfunction and brain damage is that there are often fewer obvious consequences of minimal brain dysfunction than of tumors or lesions, which result in dramatic behavioral changes. A major characteristic in differentiating between minimal brain dysfunction and the kind of brain damage that affects the person's behavior in more dramatic ways is the responsiveness of minimal brain dysfunction to educational and psychological treatment, without the need for extensive medical intervention. With the help of special teaching approaches, the person may be able to learn some form of compensation whereby other learning can occur and thus be able to lead a normal life.

The police officer may find that case histories or school histories of specific adolescents include some reference to minimal brain dysfunction or other neurological difficulties. This information could alarm the officer and imply that the individual has some sort of brain damage, which the officer might relate to the individual's delinquent behavior. In cases where such diagnosis has not been made by a qualified medical specialist, it should be assumed that the problem is an educational or psychological problem rather than one of actual brain damage. The term minimal brain dysfunction, when used by an educational specialist or psychologist, usually refers to developmental and learning behaviors that *suggest* some neurological problem rather than represent an actual medical diagnosis of such a problem. In such a case, the police officer should consult local medical specialists for a clarification of the adolescent's actual physical status.

In education and psychology, minimal brain dysfunction is associated with specific areas of language difficulty that do not cause general problems for the adolescent in learning or behavior. Such problems include inability to articulate or express oneself. Some children have difficulty expressing themselves because of anxiety, poor self-concept, fear, or poor learning. In other cases, a child's neurological development may preclude effective communication skill development. A general classification of such difficulties includes aphasia. The aphasic individual, although he may be able to understand what is said, is unable to effectively formulate words to express his own ideas. Other forms of aphasia may affect the indvidual's ability to understand speech.

The police officer should consult school and case histories for a more definitive record and explanation or medical and psychological personnel who can properly evaluate the adolescent at the time of incarceration.

Other language disabilities include reading disorders in which the adolescent has normal intelligence but is unable to learn effective reading skills. This individual may appear illiterate when asked to read or write his name, but in conversation he may exhibit adequate or even superior intelligence. There are many disabilities related to language learning, such as specific memory disorders, sequential memory disorders, and poor written expression. Some resources in this area are listed in the additional readings.

Language disabilities, because of their relationship to comprehension and expression, can cause behaviors characteristic of drug responses, seizures, or other more severe difficulties. The officer must recognize these possibilities when confronted by adolescents. A hasty assumption that an individual is drunk or has a drug problem may prevent the officer from effectively dealing with the individual.

Learning disabilities

Learning disabilities is a general term for a wide range of developmental and learning problems that prevent or inhibit children from learning effectively in school. Language disabilities are learning disabilities. However, other difficulties are also classified under this term. Children may have visual problems, perceptual-motor disorders, or specific brain injury sustained at birth or prenatally that can result in minimal developmental difficulties. These developmental difficulties can subsequently cause problems in the learning process.

Ingestion of drugs during pregnancy can affect the developing fetus in a variety of ways. Neurological development can be inhibited or even altered. Effects range from specific central nervous system damage that can affect eventual language or perceptual-motor development to difficulties in processing protein or various nutrients in the brain. These difficulties may be so subtle that they go undetected until the child reaches school age. Children who have sustained prenatal or postnatal damage make up a substantial number of the children later identified in school as having learning disabilities. There are many special services, teaching techniques, and programs that can partially or totally counteract the effects of such damage if employed early in a child's development or school career.

Many children suffer developmental difficulties as a consequence of cultural deprivation or poor parenting in the early years of development. Although such difficulties seem less serious than those caused by actual brain damage, the *consequences* are often the same. Again, early school and medical intervention can often offset the effects of deprivation and even child abuse.

The police officer may wonder why he needs to be aware of these problems, since he will not be able to identify such difficulties on the street or effect any dramatic change in adolescents with neurological or cultural problems. However, if the officer is aware that early traumas in the child's life can affect learning, he will better understand why certain children may rebel after years of school failure. There is an indirect, and often direct, relationship between the delinquent youth's deviant behavior and his early learning or developmental difficulties. Furthermore, such knowledge disputes the old idea that environment is the primary cause of juvenile delinquency. There are many physical and developmental causes that can eventuate in negative and antisocial attitudes leading to delinquent acts. The child does not often know that he has a specific developmental problem and may assume that he is simply "stupid" or that the world does not understand him. This places him in a counterposition to home and school authority as he internalizes his failure, attributing it not to some developmental difficulty but to his lack of worth or competence. Faced with failure and conflict in school and community, the adolescent may strike out through delinquent acts.

An emerging body of research suggests that many delinquents could be rehabilitated with the proper remedial education and counseling. These children, such studies assume, do not have personality disorders but have been unable to overcome their difficulty in learning or adjusting. The police officer must realize that such children will be negative, abusive, and unwilling to change because their behavior constitutes, atypical as it is, an adjustment or adaptation to their problems. If one cannot succeed in the usual way, one may have to choose available routes of adjusting that may be antisocial and delinquent.

Diabetes and hypoglycemia

Diabetes, like epilepsy, is a disorder well known by name to most of the population; however, few people have a basic understanding of its actual nature. Most people know someone who is diabetic and takes insulin to control the disorder. Less known to most people is the fact that children and adolescents also often suffer from diabetes. *Hypoglycemia,*

101

an associated disorder, has gained much publicity in recent years. We will discuss both of these disorders briefly in reference to their relationship to adolescent behavior.

Diabetes is a disorder in blood sugar, or glucose, regulation caused by a variety of conditions. Insulin, produced in the pancreas, helps to control the level of glucose in the blood; blood glucose is the primary energy source for operation of the physical system, particularly the brain and central nervous system. If insulin is not produced in the right amounts, the blood glucose level is affected, usually elevated. Symptoms of high blood glucose levels range from irritability to passiveness to coma. Children who are diabetic often pose significant problems to parents, teachers, and physicians, since proper insulin dosage, exercise, diet, and rest are all extremely important to the mental and physical health of the individual with diabetes. Changing needs for blood glucose in the active child and the physical changes of adolescence pose difficult problems in regulating the amount of insulin.

One consequence of diabetes in children and adolescents is their own emotional reaction to the disorder. Helping the child to learn, throughout his younger years; to take increasing responsibility for his own medication and treatment can be difficult. Some children and adolescents react negatively to the restrictions placed on them, whereas others become passive and defeatist. In the child who has parental or home problems and learning problems at school, emotional stress can significantly affect diabetic reactions. Thus, it is not surprising to find that some children with diabetes end up in confrontation with police, and it is important for police to recognize characteristic diabetic reactions when observing juvenile behavior. Of course, when a youth is incarcerated by the legal system, case histories and medical histories are extremely important.

An associated disorder is hypoglycemia. Hypoglycemia is a condition in which blood glucose is low and can occur as a consequence of nutritional deficiencies or temporary blood chemistry and endocrinological dysfunction. Adolescents, whose diets are often inadequate, may develop a variety of nutritional deficiencies that affect blood glucose. If an adolescent is disposed to blood glucose problems, high concentrations of sugar in the diet may precipitate frequent shifts in glucose levels. This variation can affect behavior. When the bloodstream is flooded with sugar, the body may react with lowered production of glucose, effectively shutting down energy production. A period of temporary high energy results from the ingested sugars, followed by a shortage of glucose produced by the body. In a short time, the level of blood glucose drops, and the individual is plunged into a depressive state associated with low blood glucose. The adolescent, like the police officer who eats a large lunch, may feel drowsy and lethargic. Some forms of hypoglycemia involve this fluctuation in blood glucose level, although the individual does not have diabetes. Low blood glucose levels may also cause irritability and, in some cases, extremely hostile and aggressive behavior. Restoration of the appropriate blood glucose level can cause dramatic changes in behavior, with the individual becoming more calm, social, and receptive to interaction.

Hypoglycemia has been greatly overdiagnosed in recent years because of the popularization of the syndrome in widely read literature. Many individuals who feel irritable or have difficulties concentrating on tasks or maintaining family or social relationships suspect that their problem is poor blood glucose balance. This is most often not the case, and the behavioral problems can be related to many other factors. However, in adolescence, with all of the attendant changes in physiological structure and dietary inadequacies, it is quite likely that behavioral problems can be related to temporary blood glucose problems. The police officer should be aware that, although an adolescent may not have diabetes or hypoglycemia, it is very possible that temporary blood glucose problems can exist that never reach the critical levels where they are medically diagnosed as actual disorders.

Other biochemical disorders

In recent years, there has been an increasing interest in the relationship of biochemistry and behavior. The research has taken several directions, including the study of difficulty in neurotransmission caused by biochemical disorders, nutritional deficiencies, and allergic responses. All of these directions have yielded research that suggests a more important relationship between biochemical function and behavior than was thought to exist. Psychological and sociological research has so dominated thought concerning disturbed or criminal behavior in the past 30 to 50 years that little interest has been generated in probable causal relationships between biochemical functions in the body and central nervous system and such behavior. Furthermore, a lack of adequate knowledge of biochemical function and the traditional conservatism of medical practice have both inhibited development of biochemical-behavioral relationships. Today, however, many researchers are breaking with tradition and challenging many of the accepted social and personality theories of deviant behavior.

Drug therapy has liberated millions with mental illness from institutions or at least made possible more normal life styles within institutions. Although much of the original research on medication and mental illness was designed primarily to develop a means of controlling behavior, further study has demonstrated that many medications, including vitamins, have dramatic effects on behavior. Biochemical deficiencies are presently being shown to be the basis for disorders ranging from headaches to criminal or disturbed behavior. Although the research is quite controversial, there is a continually growing body of evidence that suggests that a significant number of behavioral problems can be directly related to vitamin deficiencies or to an incapacity of the body to assimilate certain nutrients. For example, deficiencies in the vitamin B complex may be a cause of irritability and mental disorganization and prevent the assimilation of other nutrients needed for effective behavioral adjustment. Niacin has been used to change behavior in severely disturbed individuals, and megadoses of other vitamins are presently being used experimentally by psychiatrists around the country as a form of treatment in place of drug therapy, with scattered but significant successes.

There is also increasing interest in subtle food allergies that result in behavior ranging from hyperactivity or tantrums and aggression to reactions similar to those exhibited by individuals using drugs. The problem of allergic reactions to foods is growing with the increased use of artificial food colorings, additives, and preservatives in food. Many researchers are approaching this field cautiously, but most agree that there is probably some relationship between the quality of food consumed and certain forms of behavioral deviancy.

The police officer, although not a specialist in biophysical dysfunction, must be aware of its potential for influencing the behavior of delinquent youth. The approach to adolescent crime in the coming years will probably include an increasing amount of research concerning possible biophysical causes of behavioral disorders. Little can be done by the police officer at this time except to be aware that we can no longer explain delinquent behavior solely as a consequence of poor home environment or school failure. This knowledge should broaden the officer's appreciation of the needs of adolescents.

SEX HORMONES AND BEHAVIOR

One of the most controversial areas of interest today in human behavior is that of sex-related behaviors. There is a raging debate over the causal basis for sexual stereotypes. Some specialists, particularly those in sociological fields, feel that sexual stereotypes are primarily a reflection of social and cultural conditioning. This group feels that women are more nurturing, sensitive, and emotional and less aggressive than men primarily as a result of sex role stereotypes and parental, school, and societal expectations. These professionals think that women are feminine because that is what our culture expects and allows. Conversely, there are other professionals in a variety of fields who suggest that, although culture does reinforce specific behaviors for each sex, these behaviors are based on physiological and genetic differences. This second group says that we are first responsive to basic physiological conditions and that the resulting tendencies are then reinforced by cultural expectations.

Our experience and research tends to support the second group of professionals. There is a difference in chromosomal structure between men and women. Studies have demonstrated that abnormal combinations of male and female sex chromosomes can produce dramatic behavioral manifestations. Some studies have shown that overly aggressive and criminally oriented men may display an abnormal, female to male cellular chromosomal structure, a finding that supports the theory that basic cellular structure as a consequence of genetic factors can affect the behavior of the individual. Many studies concerning the effects of prenatal androgens, or male hormones, have shown dramatic although inconclusive results. Androgens appear to affect the development of physical characteristics of the fetus, and subsequent behavioral effects have also been noted. Girls who experience an overproduction of androgens before birth often display masculine behavioral characteristics during childhood and adolescence. They may be less nurturing, less interested in playing mother with dolls, more interested in functional, masculine clothes, and more aggressive and may display more interest in playing with toys usually considered appropriate for boys. Underproduction of androgens appears to have the reverse effect on boys; they display a higher degree of sensitivity, more interest in toys appropriate for girls, a lack of aggressiveness, and a tendency to enjoy playing with girls more than with boys.

The changes in behavior during the menstrual cycle are well known. As levels of female hormones fluctuate, women tend to display differing temperaments, ranging from feminine and nurturing to aggressive and negative. There have been studies in which hormonal treatment of homosexuals and lesbians has reversed the sexual tendencies of the individual. The treatment of homosexual men with male hormones sometimes tends to decrease their interest in the same sex and increase their interest in the opposite sex. Hormonal treatment is highly complex and cannot, by itself, change long-standing sexual behaviors; however, the fact that hormonal therapy can have an effect on behavior suggests the potentially important role of physiological or hormonal factors.

In the future, various forms of therapy may be developed to alter the deviant behavior of individuals who are unable to change their behavior because of its physiological basis. Again, masculine and aggressive women and effeminate and submissive men who find their sex differences important to their adjustment may develop criminal or deviant behavior in order to adjust in the culture. With the possibility that hormonal therapy can alter the underlying condition that contributes

105

to their delinquency, there may be hope of effectively rehabilitating certain criminals and delinquents whose rehabilitation is impossible through conventional approaches.

The police officer has to add still another range of behavioral possibilities for delinquent behavior to the simplistic idea that "bad kids come from bad homes." It is unlikely that a complete endocrinological examination will be done on every adolescent who is in trouble with the law. However, an awareness of the possibility of this type of dysfunction puts the officer in a better position to observe and evaluate the behavior of adolescents who have difficulties.

Some studies suggest that sex hormone–related behavioral problems can stem from dysfunction in other areas of the glandular system. Dysfunction of the thyroid can produce irritability, anxiety, and bizarre thoughts, as in dysfunction of other important glands. It would seem reasonable to expect that, as the child moves into the period of increased hormonal and glandular change of early adolescence, there would be an increased possibility for endocrinological disturbances, at least on a temporary basis. Traditionally, endocrinologists have been more concerned with the physical effects of glandular dysfunction than possible hormone-related behavioral changes that may be associated with long-term or temporary changes in physical function.

SUMMARY

During adolescence, many physiological changes occur in a short time; thus, it is not surprising that some researchers are looking for possible behavioral effects of these changes in children who are particularly vulnerable. Children who have existed on substandard diets, who ingest drugs both directly and as part of their daily food intake, and who have various nutritional deficiencies that often plague the underprivileged may become adolescents who are more vulnerable to potential difficulties during this period of dramatic physiological change.

We conclude this chapter with a reminder that this brief overview of nonsociological factors in adolescent behavior is at best tentative. Awareness and understanding of neurological, physiological, and endocrinological effects on behavior are growing in the related areas of research. The police officer does not have adequate medical resources to assist him in making the needed evaluation of adolescent behavior. However, as more information is gathered about child and adolescent development, the alert police officer will be able to integrate it into his approach to adolescent crime and delinquency. The more limited sociological concepts used in the past not only fail to explain criminal behavior but may, in fact, reduce our ability to alter the nature of crime in this country.

REFERENCE

1. Eissier, K. R. (Ed.) *Searchlight on delinquency.* New York: International Universities Press, 1949, p. 3.

ADDITIONAL READINGS

Bakin, H., & Bakin, R. *Behavior disorders in children.* Philadelphia: W. B. Saunders, 1972.

Cheraskin, E., & Ringsdorf, W. M., Jr., with Brecher, A. *Psychodietetics.* New York: Bantam, 1974.

Fincger, J. *Human intelligence.* New York: G. P. Putnam's Sons, 1976.

Friedman, R., Richart, R., & Wiele, R. *Sex differences in behavior.* New York: Wiley Biomedical Health Publication, 1976.

Lerner, J. *Children with learning disabilities.* Boston: Houghton Mifflin, 1976.

Newbold, H. L. *Mega-nutrients: for your nerves.* New York: Wyden, 1975.

Passwater, R. *Supernutrition.* New York: Dial Press, 1975.

Pfeiffer, C. *Mental and elemental nutrients: A physician's guide to nutrition and health care.* New Canaan, Conn.: Keats, 1975.

Schrag, P., & Divoky, D. *The myth of the hyperactive child.* New York: Pantheon, 1975.

CHAPTER 7

CONFRONTATION
WITH THE LAW

You can preach, tell, threaten, and demand,
But I am the one who is sixteen.

This book is about adolescence and problems associated with adolescence in relation to delinquency and crime, rather than about crime, poverty, or the problem of law enforcement. The law enforcement officer receives much training and is often involved in problems relating to crime. Our concern here is how, in the course of adolescent development, individuals come into contact with the law. Whereas many other aspects of adolescence have been previously discussed in this book, this chapter is devoted to some comments concerning the specific situations in which an adolescent may come into contact with the legal system and the officer who must enforce the laws. Hopefully, a better understanding of the adolescent and the difficulties that he encounters will assist the officer in better understanding the individual he faces. This should benefit both the officer and the adolescent. The topics that we will deal with are some of the most difficult and require much study and experience in law enforcement. Additional readings will be listed at the end of the chapter for those officers who wish to pursue further the topics reviewed.

The laws governing juvenile behavior are generally both protective and restrictive; in many cases a juvenile can be held for acts that are not considered crimes when committed by adults but are considered inappropriate and dangerous to the welfare of the adolescent. Juvenile delinquency, as we have come to label the conduct of persons under a fixed, statutory age who violate the law, consists of the following according to R. W. Kobetz:

1. Those forms of behavior which would be called crime if engaged in by adults.
2. Those noncriminal but symptomatic behavioral patterns which most persons believe tend to direct the child into antisocial channels. Smoking, truancy, curfew violations, runaways, and similar offenses, although not in the strict sense considered to be criminal acts, are part of selective legislative definition of behavior which is considered unhealthy for the development of a child.[1]

Many states are currently altering their juvenile codes and working toward a more just and liberal system of meeting the needs of both the courts and the child. The actions of the courts and the law enforcement agency in status offenses and various criminal acts are being reviewed in an attempt to more justly and efficiently manage the growing numbers and complexity of juvenile offenses.

THE RUNAWAY

In recent years an increasing number of adolescents run rather than resist. They may begin by simply refusing to come home one night and progress to eventually leaving altogether. They may simply pick up and leave after school one day and not be seen for some time. Runaways come from all economic groups, from urban and rural areas, and they are both boys and girls. There are many reasons for runaway behavior, ranging from severe psychological personal problems to escape from brutal and sadistic parents. Adolescents run from themselves and from their parents or the world that somehow fails them. They run from the boredom of schools and from the persecution of an unjust economic and social system that oppresses them, and they run in search of security, hope, and opportunity. They can be classified by sex, by age, and by economic status, and they can be classified according to behavior. As a group they may have many things in common, but one thing is usually true: Every runaway has a uniqueness within himself and his dilemma and must be treated individually.

Many adolescents, when facing the identity crisis and the age of discontinuity, find that running away is a "reasonable" out from a situation that offers them no direction. We have seen many runaways not only in the clinic but on the streets, in special places of refuge ranging from dingy houses in the inner city to garages of friends who live in distant towns. One of the most common characteristics of the runaway is a lack of school and parent communication and understanding of the needs of the adolescent. Many runaways are gang and delinquency oriented and come from economically deprived areas, but an increasing number of runaways come from the middle class, from the "good" communities, the bedroom communities of families struggling for something more. It is often easier to understand the adolescent who runs from poverty and oppression than the individual who seems to "have it all." The "Jesus freaks," the "Moonies," and strange occult groups all appear to attract adolescents who are searching for something, regardless of economic background. It is a search for something that we would assume to be available in their home or school or in another institution in the community. It is not.

The rebel, who is attempting to identify himself as an individual through severe rebellion against authority, often runs away as a means of breaking with the traditions of his past. These adolescents often run to causes, to groups who are in some way organized to effectively fight the establishment. In the mild case, the adolescent joins a commune, whereas in more deviant cases he joins a Manson family and commits unbelievable crimes against society. They see themselves not attacking a victim but the "system" to call attention to a need for change. The rebellious adolescent who joins a commune or religious movement may be able, in time, to return to his life and community and pick up the pieces. The individual who, during this stage of discontinuity and confusion, becomes involved with a truly criminal movement may become increasingly less responsive to intervention. However, the rebel is not really seeking criminality or deviancy. Eventual readjustment into the mainstream of society is possible.

In many cases, the parents of the rebel and the schools are as much a factor in their dilemma as their own confusion. Many of today's parents maintain a double standard. They are caught up in "getting ahead," they worship material things, and their values reflect the competitive model of modern society. The adolescent is in the stage of life that precedes assimilation of these values. He is at that point where "self" and finding one's own identity are most important. Therefore, living out the conditioned and sterile life styles of his parents may seem impossible and depersonalized. Parents and educators moralize and attempt to direct his behavior into the "right" paths. To the adolescent who feels lost and totally helpless and is screaming for help, such counsel sounds like a summary of *1984*. The school becomes little more than an institution and not a very personalized one. The increasing size of schools and the trend toward tighter discipline and depersonalization have left many adolescents to fend for themselves, unable to find that special teacher or counselor who might reach out to them and give some direction. It is at this point that many adolescents take their first drug trip, not because they want drugs but because they want to find feeling or meaning within themselves. With the taking of drugs, which is primarily a social tool for gangs and groups, there is a feeling of euphoria, a feeling of knowing, being, and belonging. The use of drugs involves many rituals. One must learn how to enjoy the sensation of the drug. One must have instruction and go through initiation rites to become a trusted member of a group. Alienation from parents and teachers is the weapon against the adolescent's feeling of hopelessness, and drugs and the drug group provide the means of escape and an opportunity for belonging and finding purpose.

Following alienation, drug use, and membership in deviant gangs, the individual becomes increasingly convinced of the crime and hypocrisy of the adult world. The next step is to run, for there are "friends" all over the country who "understand."

The neurotic adolescent, who already feels anxious and has an extended history of worry, illness, and uncertainty, often finds running away a potential way of solving his problem, although he seldom knows what his problem is. The neurotic adolescent reaches for security and a sense of well-being. Like the follower, he is a prime target for the pseudoreligious groups. These two individuals, one insecure and anxiety ridden and the other dependent, find comfort in the strict and disciplined external controls of radical religious groups. They are ready to accept any doctrine or direction that will make them feel secure and purposeful. Once indoctrinated with the beliefs of a special "family,"

111

religious group, or organization, they can become fanatic advocates of the organization, acting out the group goals without regard for themselves. They become immersed in the organization, the "great leader," or the religion, and they act much like zombies in horror movies. They may even commit murder or other serious crimes under the direction of the leader. Whereas the rebel may take the direction of special groups that are action oriented, the neurotic adolescent and the follower often join groups that will control and provide for them. They have no need to find a great cause, unlike the rebel; they simply want peace and security.

Psychotic and schizoid individuals may run away for extremely serious reasons. They are unable to sort out their world, and they run without regard for direction or purpose. They range from the individual who believes that he is the reincarnation of God to the individual who fantasizes himself as a great criminal. Their delusions and separation of feeling and thought make them both dangerous to others and to themselves. Criminal behavior is less likely than some bizarre and often fruitless act in which all suffer.

The psychotic individual may run, but his inability to organize himself and to adequately comprehend the reality of his environment makes him unlikely to maintain his runaway status long, before he is detained by some agency or law officer. However, he is capable of becoming involved in a variety of crimes and deviant behaviors before being detained.

The primitive and unsocialized runaway is often escaping from poverty, abuse from parents, or school. He is likely to be successful at running because his level of existence at home may be little better and even worse than living in the streets. The unsocialized individual's background and history make him likely to turn to criminal behavior, because he may see little reason not to steal or maintain himself through other criminal means. This individual represents the traditional runaway of a time before running away became nationally prominent or the social thing to do during the summer. Children have run away from poor homes for years, but it never drew much attention. Few really cared much about the poor.

The unsocialized individual might run away to another city, but often he simply runs to a friend's across town, to an aunt, or to the home of an absent father for a short time before being returned by some member of the family. Too often poor children are a burden already, and a temporary absence is not always so important. This is not to say that the poor do not care for their children, but under poverty conditions there is more possibility of poor child supervision and care. In any case, runaway children did not become a focus of national attention until recently, when the runaway problem began to affect the middle class and, therefore, the power and political or social structure of the country. However, the motivation of the poor child who runs away is usually quite different from that of the middle class runaway and more urgent.

CHILD ABUSE AND THE ADOLESCENT

Child abuse, like the problem of the runaway, seems to be related to contemporary society but is an old problem that affects a greater portion of the population today than it once did. A major obstacle in the prevention of child abuse has been difficulty in reporting of cases, either by the families or professionals who may have suspected probable abuse. Physicians and agencies who become aware of possible child abuse are hampered by the fine line between prevention of child abuse and infringement of a parent's rights as an individual. Child abuse may be difficult to prove; both individuals and agencies have had difficulty getting cases to court. This continues to be a law enforcement problem, although recent coverage by health agencies, law enforcement agencies, and the media has made the public more aware of the problem. The number of cases of child abuse being reported and in which some legal action ensues is increasing.

Child abuse relates to adolescence in two ways. Adolescents, like children, are abused by their parents, and adolescents abuse their own children when young couples are psychologically unprepared for the responsibilities of parenting. We believe that the problem of abuse of adolescents is more widespread than that of abuse of children by adolescents, since the number of adolescents who may be abused is much greater than the number who have children of their own.

Abuse of adolescents can take many forms, ranging from physical abuse, particularly of girls, to psychological and sexual abuse. When the adolescent enters the period of discontinuity between childhood and adulthood, he is extremely vulnerable to stress and to actions. The emerging adult appearance of the adolescent in itself can cause ambivalent feelings in parents. As the adolescent attempts to establish himself as a person instead of a child, parents sometimes find great difficulty in accepting this change. In some families, this period of discontinuity for the adolescent is also a period of confusion and revelation for the parents. They have never had an adolescent before, and at times emotions can range from anxiety to anger. The adolescent begins to test the limits of childhood, and the parent has to readjust his perception of this new person in the house. This period of adjustment is not always easy, although most families move through it with a minimum of difficulty. For the families who do not find the transition smooth, many difficulties can ensue.

Parents may attempt to continue to maintain total control over the adolescent. If this control is not replaced by reasonable expectations and sharing of responsibility with the adolescent, conflict can result. A father may become so frustrated that talking no longer is adequate and he strikes out at his daughter or son. Brutal physical punishment can occur, although at some point the adolescent is likely to escape from the home. If the adolescent returns and some adjustments are made, he may continue at home and school with a renewed understanding and even family unity. However, if the parents continue to maintain attitudes of rejection and control, accompanied by the possibility of physical abuse, then the adolescent may leave for good and join the ranks of the runaways.

Physical abuse as a consequence of adolescent-parent conflict is not uncommon. However, the manner in which parents and adolescents handle this conflict depends on many factors, including culture, community, the mental health of the individuals involved, relatives, and other individuals in the community who may counsel one or all of the family members. The more isolated the family from relatives, the more severe their economic plight, and the lower the level of family unity and interaction before the conflict, the more likely it is that the adolescent will run or fight. One can never predict the results of adolescent abuse because of the many factors involved. However, certain factors are critical. Some conditions that prevent or tend to lessen the severity of adolescent-parent conflict follow:

1. The ability of family members to continue communication during and following conflict.
2. The ability of the parents to be flexible enough to recognize, perhaps for the first time, that the adolescent is maturing and that their attitudes and management of the adolescent must change toward a parent role of guidance rather than control.
3. The ability and willingness of the parents and the adolescent to regroup and work the problems out, either by themselves or with outside professional help.
4. The ability of the parents or an outside resource to reduce tension, establish new means of communication, and develop guidelines for behavior.
5. The ability of the parents and the adolescent to maintain school, community, and family roles that are productive during the period of readjustment.
6. The willingness of the adolescent to accept continued parental limits and to begin to set personal educational, training, and occupational goals in order to secure eventual independence.

It is easy to see that these conditions may be impossible to maintain if family structure and culture work against such development and resolution of the problem. In cases where the family is not a stable reference group for the adolescent, he may choose one of several directions that

114

seem, at his stage of development, to be logical solutions. These include:

1. Running away
2. Involvement in delinquent acts and groups as a means of generalizing hostility toward parents and authority
3. Suicide
4. Drug involvement
5. Depression and apathy

Adolescent abuse in the form of parental rejection; physical abuse; psychological abuse, such as humiliation, severe restrictions, and withdrawal of privileges; and increased punitiveness, that is, constant questioning, "nagging," and accusations, all magnify the adolescent's difficulties and tend to drive him to one of the foregoing reactions. In extreme cases, an adolescent may even want to kill one or both parents.

Abuse by parents is perhaps one of the most frequent factors in these reactions. This abuse is not limited to lower-class families as many believe but occurs in nearly all economic and cultural groups. Abuse does occur in the middle and upper classes, but the ability of these groups to acquire help and the ability of the family to readjust are often greater than in the lower economic classes. Often the middle and upper economic groups can afford more alternatives and resources by which the problem may be resolved.

Another causal factor in these reactions is that of peer group and school, or the combined social and cultural environment of the adolescent. The adolescent who is not doing well in school, who finds it difficult to make or keep friends, or who has a history of personal difficulties may react to the depersonalization of groups and school in much the same manner in which he reacts to parents who are abusive. The lack of realistic programs for the underachiever and the marginal student, the lack of counselors available for counseling at a personal level, the unwillingness of teachers to reach out to the student, and the lack of adequate community and school evening and weekend activities for adolescents all contribute to the dilemma of the adolescent who needs help. Few adolescents wish to become delinquent or engage in severe antisocial behavior. Conditions cause the adolescent to choose one of these ways out of their dilemma. In most cases, adolescents do not choose to become delinquent but are driven into it by their culture, parents, and school.

For the individual who is responding to adolescence in a rebellious way, running away or becoming involved in delinquent groups may provide the needed outlet for frustration and anger, whereas the neurotic individual may choose running away, suicide, or drug involvement or may become depressed and apathetic, requiring mental health intervention. The psychotic or schizoid individual may choose any of the listed

115

reactions; primitive and unsocialized adolescents are more apt to run away, become involved in delinquent groups, use drugs, or even engage in impulsive homicide. In all cases, the most important preventative factor is communication. Communication involves talking to the individual and helping him substitute verbal interaction for physical or emotional responses. It matters little whether this assistance comes from a parent, a teacher, a friend, or a police officer; verbal interaction and reasoning are the substitutes for physical aggression and psychological deterioration. If an individual ever needs love, understanding, and support, it is during adolescence, when he first struggles to become a person in his own right.

There are certain indicators that might suggest to the officer that he is dealing with abusive parents or abused children. The following list is far from inclusive but should help the officer to isolate the problem he is confronting. No single characteristic should be isolated as an indicator; the lists should be considered as behavioral clusters.

CHARACTERISTICS OF ABUSIVE PARENTS

1. Insecure
2. Inability to show affection
3. Lack of self-worth
4. Belief that children should be punished for failures
5. Unrealistic expectations placed on children
6. Were abused themselves as children
7. Parent/child needs don't coincide
8. Belief that punishment has educational value
9. No establishment of basic trust by parents
10. Few things child does win parent's approval
11. Unpredictable behavior
12. Delay unduly in getting child help
13. Believe child is property of parents

PHYSICAL INDICES OF ABUSED CHILDREN

1. Hungry
2. Poorly clothed
3. Unkempt
4. Poor skin color
5. Listless
6. Nonverbal communication
7. Bruises in various stages of healing
8. Welts and burns
9. Evidence of repeated injury
10. Evidence of repeated fractures

BEHAVIORAL INDICES OF ABUSED CHILDREN

1. Overly compliant
2. Passive
3. Undemanding behavior aimed at maintaining a low profile

116

4. Avoids confrontation that may lead to further abuse
5. Capacity to become extremely aggressive
6. Demanding and rageful behavior caused by continual frustration
7. Overly adaptive behavior in response to unresolved needs of parent
8. Lags in development
9. Temper tantrums
10. Short attention span
11. Appears fearful[2]

It is a common belief that the child who is abused will often become a child abuser in adulthood. This may be true, but the problem is far more complex than the idea of the abused learning abuse through experience or modeling. One must talk with, listen to, and understand the feelings and problems of the child abuser before an appreciation of the complexity of the problem can be gained. Much of the current literature on child abuse tends to stress general culture and social behavior training as the problems behind child abuse. As one delves into the literature and meets with parents, particularly teenaged parents, one finds that there are many more facets to the problem than might be imagined.

Being a parent requires far more than merely conceiving a child, being married, or feeling responsible as a human being. Parenting is influenced by the inner feelings of the parents as individuals, the nature of their relationship, their own family background, situational economic and social conditions, personal stress and problems, and education. There are many traditional pitfalls of marriage and parenting that can cause various forms of child abuse. The couple who conceives merely to have someone to love, someone they hope will love them back, is displaying immature thinking. The child who never received love from parents who may have been very punitive and rejecting is a logical candidate for attempting to find this love somewhere. The problem is that these children have never learned the mutuality and responsibility or behaviors involved in being a parent. As infant care becomes a burden and the infant demands what seems more love than he can give back, the mother may become depressed, feel rejected, and eventually become hostile to her own child. The father, who married because of circumstances of opportunity or periods of seemingly intense and "everlasting" love, without the maturity or responsibility to give of himself to others, may find the infant's crying and constant demands on his wife's time so irritating that he displays aggressive behavior toward the infant. For parents who conceive before they are financially able to provide for a child, the subsequent economic and social limitations placed on their relationship can cause hostility that is focused on the infant. Such parents may abandon their child or give it away temporarily. The mother who comes from a deprived family and must seek continual employment to survive may find the infant an increasing burden. She may leave the infant with her own parents, who may be battering adults, resentful of both the infant and the mother's marriage. The girl who conceives out of wedlock, or is rejected by her parents, or whose husband only comes home occasionally to get money or spend a few hours in love making before disappearing again is likely to become a child abuser. The father or mother who has some sort of personality disorder that is eventually expressed through sadistic and punitive behavior toward the child is not uncommon. These are only examples of the many circumstances, both traditional and unusual, that create conditions for child abuse, neglect, or abandonment. They are all manifestations of potential behaviors of the adolescent period, when the individual has not resolved his own needs and is less able to serve the needs of another.

SEXUAL ABUSE

Sexual abuse is most often defined as sexual advances, involvement, or interaction between an adolescent girl and her father, although other family members or relatives may be involved. Sexual abuse, such as rape, is difficult to prove because of the hesitancy of the girl to report the incident or seek assistance. With the increased emphasis on rape and management of rape cases, the number of incest cases reported is also increasing. The women's movement and encouragement of equality for women in all areas of life are also contributing to increased reporting of incest cases. For much of the middle class, incest is something that is not thought of, and it is assumed to be a problem associated only with families in disadvantaged areas. This may be generally true, but the occurrence of incest in the middle and upper classes is greater than most people would think.

In many cases of incest, the father is drunk at the time. In others, the father claims that the girl acted provocatively, or a stepdaughter is involved. A stepfather may feel he has license to commit incest since the girl is not a blood relative. Certainly, in the primitive and unsocialized man the potential for incest is greater because of his lack of socialization, of impulse control, and of a value system that would preclude such behavior. Other relatives may be involved in child molestation and incest for many of the same reasons.

The responses of the adolescent girl to incest can be varied. In most cases, however, the girl is fearful, ashamed, and psychologically disoriented. She may not tell her mother, and frequently she is unable to tell anyone. The psychological effects may be long lasting or even permanent, retarding normal sexual development and eventual establishment of adequate sexual relationships. In some cases of incest, as in rape, the girl needs special assistance and, if possible, a complete physical examination and medical intervention.

118

RAPE

Rape has become the focus of increased community and police attention, with the development of many special programs and police groups who work with this problem nearly exclusively.

There are four basic types of blame models commonly used to describe the cause of rape: victim blame, offender blame, societal blame, and situational blame. Victim blame is common among men: the woman is characterized as displaying seductive or sexual behaviors and dress. Offender blame is used in relation to an individual described as driven by overwhelming lust and aggression. This model is popular in the single girl fear syndrome. Societal blame finds reasons for the act of rape in the many ills and fundamental problems of our culture. Situational blame suggests that dark alleys, passive women, overcrowding, and a host of other problems of a particular location create the conditions and probability of rape.

One problem in understanding rape is the difficulty of finding a specific psychological type of individual who is likely to be a rapist. As in many of the behaviors previously discussed, the assailant has few characteristics that could be classified into neat personality types or kinds of social conditions that might be conducive to rape. Furthermore, prosecution of the assailant is difficult even with substantial evidence, because judges and juries often suspect a woman of leading her assailant on or of indirectly encouraging him. This is one of the fears of the rape victim, although the evidence may illustrate that she was forcibly raped. In the final analysis, will anyone believe her?

Rape is forced, violent sexual penetration against a victim's will and without the victim's consent. According to Burgess and Holmstrom, most rape victims develop a rape trauma syndrome. The trauma syndrome is a reaction to a life-threatening situation and includes an acute phase of disorganization in the victim's life style. In a study completed by Burgess and Holmstrom, 79% of all rape victims admitted to the Boston City Hospital displayed this syndrome. A second group, including 5% of all sexual assault victims admitted to the hospital, was identified as accessory-to-sex victims. These victims had been pressured into sexual activity by a person who, because of their age or authority, had power over them. A final group reported in this study was made up of victims of sex-stress situations in which both parties had initially consented. This group composed 16% of the total number of sexual assault victims at the hospital.[3]

Obtaining agreement on the actual classification of a case involving rape is often a nightmare for law enforcement agencies. Not only the public appears to have difficulty in passing judgment while sitting on a jury; the judges have difficulty defining a specific case as rape. Judges may see an individual as a genuine victim, as in a case where the victim

119

was obviously attacked without provocation in a parking lot or apartment by a total stranger. Or the judge may call it "consensual intercourse" if he thinks the victim may have been "asking for it" by being picked up in a bar. Other cases have been attributed to "female vindictiveness," because complainants were thought to be trying to "get even" with a man.[4]

It will be a difficult task for the police officer to determine whether or not sexual abuse has taken place. Following is a list of possible indicators of sexual abuse; however, these should not be looked for singly but in a cluster to be suggestive of sexual abuse.

    A. Underlying family conditions
        1. Prolonged absence of one parent
        2. Loss of parent
        3. Severe overcrowding
        4. Lack of social and emotional contacts
        5. Geographic isolation
        6. Alcoholism
        7. Passive parent
        8. Seductive child
    B. Behavioral indicators
        1. Regression (retreat into fantasy)
        2. Delinquency or aggression
        3. Poor peer relationships
        4. Extremely protective parenting
        5. Unwillingness to participate in activities
        6. Running away
        7. Drug use and abuse
        8. Indirect allusions[2]

The adolescent and rape

During adolescence, a period of heightened sexual awareness and experimentation, petting and intercourse occur that can come uncomfortably close to rape in the mind of the girl and still be called "consensual intercourse" by a court or jury if this level of complaint is reached. Forcible rape is assumed to be that incident in which the girl is penetrated against her will. There are many adolescent girls who are probably the victims of rape by boyfriends or even casual friends. During adolescence, the young couple may find that petting goes beyond the limit; the boy pursues while the girl resists, but she eventually gives in. These incidents are not usually perceived by the girl as rape, although some may be. Such a case would not be easily accepted by legal authorities or by juries. It does not conform to the generally accepted definition of rape. The reader is reminded, however, that we are concerned here with events that occur in adolescent development, and the boy often has less inhibitions concerning sex than the girl in traditional groups.

The adolescent girl bears a large part of the responsibility for premarital intercourse because of traditional sexual stereotypes. The boy is taught to be the aggressor; our language is filled with the expressions of male sexual dominance: Men "take it," "make a conquest," "score," and "get it on." The woman is to be had, and the man is to "get it." In social and cultural conditioning, the woman is an object that the man seeks for his satisfaction. In many cultures, the man has been taught to "give pleasure" to the woman, to avoid climax so that the woman enjoys the encounter. Such cultures teach the man to assist the woman in reaching climax several times, while delaying his own climax, in order to enhance her enjoyment. However, in our culture it appears that the man's satisfaction and his demonstration of manhood through sexual conquest are central in sexual encounters. Therefore, one may view a significant number of adolescent sexual encounters as bordering on rape rather than as mutual sexual encounters. Even when a girl reports a rape, the orientation of both male and female judges and jurors often causes them to dismiss the case simply because the girl has some relationship with the boy or man. It is assumed, in these cases, that the girl in some way incited the boy to the act. Until prevalent social attitudes change relative to the basic sexual stereotypes, this problem will doubtless continue to exist. The girl is placed in a role of greater responsibility for any sexual encounter. This often surprises and depresses the girl when she begins to have sexual encounters in adolescence. Sexual behavior is a major focus of conflict and difficulties in role adjustment and learning during adolescence. Boys and girls often receive very different messages throughout childhood concerning sexual activity and roles. This creates more difficulties in adolescent development, since both boys and girls must spend much energy and time slowly working out personal beliefs about behaviors that are possibly in opposition to what they have been taught, poorly and even detrimentally, by parents and schools in childhood.

The adolescent girl who is a victim of rape as defined by the law responds in much the same manner as the woman, except that rape trauma and psychological effects of the rape can be far more profound. The adolescent girl is already vulnerable because of the usual problems encountered during adolescence. Rape can create a special trauma in adolescent girls, since they have not yet established a clear self-concept, a belief system, or a stable personal identity. Girls who experience rape in adolescence may find it difficult to return to school, to face their friends, or to assume their normal life style. Centers that are currently opening around the country to counsel the victims of rape have a special and significant role to play in assisting these girls. Some important services and responses that should be offered when a girl or her parents report rape are as follows:

121

HOTLINE OR PHONE CALLS TO REPORT RAPE

1. Provide initial contact with rape victim.
2. Obtain basic data, and record time and date of call, name of person calling if they will give it, nature of call, and time spent on call.
3. Encourage victim to come to the emergency room for treatment, and give information regarding services that will be provided.
4. Arrange transportation for victim by police if requested.

MEDICAL AND COUNSELING SERVICES ·

1. Provide immediate care, including gynecological, traumatic, psychiatric, and nursing care.
2. Provide necessary assistance and encouragement to report incident to proper law enforcement agency.
3. Provide appointments for long-term psychological care for adolescent, family, or friends, as necessary.
4. Provide instructions and necessary follow-up by medical and psychological services to assure prevention of pregnancy and control of venereal disease.

Police response to the rape victim

According to Keefe and O'Reilly, the following procedures are important in the initial response to a rape victim on the scene:

1. Avoid any suggestion of force so that the victim will not perceive you as an aggressive person.
2. Be nonjudgmental and patient. Allow her to discuss the incident willingly and naturally.
3. Use a gentle approach and encourage the victim to freely discuss the incident or her feelings.
4. Conduct the questioning at an appropriate place, usually the victim's home, or ask where she would like to talk.
5. Be equally tactful with any family members who may be present.
6. See the victim privately away from family members, and then allow family members to listen to the story to assist in clarification.
7. A victim coming to the station house alone may want support and assistance in dealing with her family. Assist in this and establish a close relationship with them.
8. In later interviews explain court procedures to her and remain with her in court.
9. If the victim specifically and spontaneously requests a female officer, one should be provided for her. In many cases today a special task force utilizing female police officers is involved in rape investigations.[5]

The cooperation of special police teams, local health and medical authorities, and mental health services is needed in the case of rape. The most significant initial problem is to provide the victim with medical and psychological assistance in order to obtain immediate physical and medical evaluations; this is for the patient's medical benefit and to acquire information that may assist in the apprehension of the rapist.

The adolescent rapist

The adolescent rapist ranges from the boy who becomes involved in drugs, alcohol, or gang behaviors to the individual who is truly disturbed or unsocialized. Attempts to describe behavioral patterns of the potential rapist are difficult with men and even more difficult with adolescents, who are in a state of tension and change.

A number of rapes occur as a gang behavior or in an informal or less organized group of adolescent boys who become engaged in a situation involving rape. Often the most critical aspect of rape is the assault and battery that occurs. Whether a solitary adolescent is involved or a gang, motivations are usually more complex than an introduction into the rites of a group or manhood. Many adolescent girls in deprived urban areas are traumatized by adolescent gangs who make it unlikely that a girl will report the incident. The number of such cases that is unreported is probably much higher than those unreported by women. The adolescent girl herself is part of the interplay of relationships within the community, and rape may be more of an "adolescent in-group" action than something that will be viewed as rape by the adolescents themselves. Furthermore, because of the girl's familiarity with the gang or individual involved, the existence of a rape case would be questioned in court. Thus, because of legal reasons and the nature of the adolescent group relationship, adolescent rape by other adolescents is a problem that is very difficult to investigate; medical and legal action is also difficult to obtain. The problems for the police officer in investigating and initiating an arrest are complex and require increased in-depth training by police trainers.

Many cases of rape of adolescent girls, including both criminal and status offenses, are associated with other delinquent acts. These cases often provoke much public reaction. The case of a girl who is raped by an adolescent during a burglary or robbery that is reported in the newspaper usually causes much public reaction, and police agencies are the recipients of much pressure and even condemnation. However, as our discussion has shown, the police and law enforcement agencies face a complex problem in the management of rape cases.

PROSTITUTION

Prostitution is a profession, a means of making money, and a way of gaining some sort of status. In our society, it is no less a crime than many other forms of deviant behavior. The teenaged girl may be introduced to prostitution by a friend, a relative, or even an adult who is looking for

123

young girls for his own business. Most frequently, however, she is introduced by another girl who is already active. It may begin with a supposed date that ends up in bed, the date having been arranged by another girl. The new initiate may not even be aware that she has agreed to a paid sexual encounter. She may even be surprised when her date gives her money. Other girls are introduced to prostitution in a more straightforward manner as a way to make money. In either case, if the girl decides to enter the field, she becomes the responsibility of the friend who initiated her. She spends a period of time learning the techniques and being monitored by her teacher, but eventually she becomes a free agent or may have her own pimp. The training period may last from several months to over a year as the trainee becomes more involved in the culture of prostitution. Prostitution may make it possible for her to enjoy a life style far beyond that which she might achieve through legitimate employment. The girl may enter prostitution as soon as she enters adolescence, presenting an attractive "target" for interested men.

Whether the girl becomes a call girl or a streetwalker depends on a number of variables, including who introduces her and the availability of clients in her neighborhood. To be a call girl is often more desirable from the girl's standpoint because of the relative safety from police detection and the nature of the work. The call girl can be more discrete, can demand higher fees, and is often able to deal with higher-class clients. The streetwalker is open to more public recognition, often meets less desirable clients, must have more "street knowledge," and in general has a rougher time being successful in her work.

When we are talking about urban areas of population, it does little good to attempt to understand from a middle-class viewpoint why a girl enters prostitution, particularly in her early adolescent years. It is a way of making money and surviving in an economic system that requires that every individual find some way to make it on his own. There have been many psychological studies of prostitutes, and the field of sociology is filled with "professionals" who take more interest in the subject than one might expect from a clinical viewpoint. These studies have explored the depths of the "culture of poverty": the broken homes and the damaging effects of living in homes where drugs, alcohol, and unemployment are a way of life. However, psychologists and sociologists have had little effect on the incidence or treatment of the problem. Prostitution means making money, having a profession, and gaining some sort of status. It is the result of many cultural and economic problems that are no closer to being resolved today than they were before either psychology or sociology became professional fields. This is not an attempt to justify prostitution or to discredit these fields. However, prostitution is a problem that cannot be dealt with through academic research alone.

The adolescent gang is sometimes the site of introduction of both boys and girls into various kinds of paid sexual activity, and today it appears that these ventures are developing into larger systems of activity. Boys are often introduced to the role of "hustler" by a gang that limits and controls the nature of the acts performed and other areas of behavior. The street hustler often performs "tricks" or fellatio with men for money, and such individuals do not think of themselves as homosexuals. They would describe "queer" individuals as those who engage in homosexual relationships for free or out of love; they see themselves as providing a service for homosexuals, although they themselves are not "fags." Like the female prostitute, these boys do not see their business as sordid, perverted, or in any way deviant. Doubtless, it is difficult for many of us to imagine not thinking of such acts as deviant, but these boys and girls have not read the book. Theirs is a way of life and a business, and their behavior is part of a complex culture in which values are very different from those of the middle class.

In many areas of the country today; picking up runaway boys and girls and introducing them to an organized ring of adolescents involved in homosexual and heterosexual prostitution comprise a growing business. Often, these adolescents are moved from state to state. To a great extent, they are prisoners, although their attitude toward their situation may range from acceptance to total disorientation and submission.

A PROBLEM OF VALUES AND CULTURE

The exploitation of adolescents for prostitution and homosexual acts is an extreme form of deviancy and criminality. It is opposed to the middle-class concept that every human being is entitled to the opportunity to live a productive and happy life. However, two perspectives exist in the matter of adolescent sexual deviancy. Many seasoned police officers are aware of the contradiction between the middle-class laws and values they must enforce and the subcultural structure within which they must attempt to enforce them. The sociologist or psychologist who studies deviancy most often researches it from the standpoint of the cultural norm, middle-class values, and a political system that makes the laws and dictates the structure of "normal" behavior. The police officer who works the streets and must deal with homosexual hustlers and adolescent prostitutes often stands between two worlds with extremely different value sytems.

There are "adjusted" and "maladjusted" prostitutes and homosexuals, just as there is a middle-class value structure and a subculture value structure. An adolescent girl may become a prostitute because of extreme feelings of inadequacy, as a reaction to rejection by her father and men in general, or because of deep-seated neurotic feelings of anger and rejection of both herself and society in general. These girls enter deviant sexual relationships as a means of dealing in some way with their psychological disabilities. It seldom works, and they end up as alcoholics, drug addicts, and hopelessly disturbed individuals. Conversely, there are prostitutes who live out their lives in a more or less adjusted way, victims of both society and their cultural background. To these girls, prostitution and other forms of deviant behavior are often as "normal" for their life styles as marriage and family are for the middle-class girl. When their youth fades and they no longer can function as prostitutes, they too may end their days in addiction, alcoholism, or severe deprivation and loneliness. This life style gives meaning to the "crime of poverty." Individuals born into this subculture are unable to rise to higher levels of adjustment and behavior, making it impossible for them to form the attitudes necessary to seek the opportunities of the middle-class girl or to learn how to organize their lives around the middle-class value structure. Culture takes its toll.

These realities may be understood by the police officer and often make his role in the profession somewhat fatalistic in later years. However, the officer must strive to maintain his or her own perspective in a contradictory world. It is difficult not to become so hardened, pessimistic, and defeated that one is unable to mobilize resources and continually try to assist the community of individuals around one in changing their behavior. Police work is difficult and requires far more than simply being well trained in law enforcement. This is seldom understood by the stable community that pays the salary of the police officer: the middle class. Social action programs, Big Brother and Sister programs, drug programs, and the many other education and service functions provided by the police department in most communities are the only means through which change can be sought, although these programs seem meager compared with the overwhelming problems facing the law enforcement officer.

HOMOSEXUALITY

For the adolescent, homosexuality is generally a stage of development rather than a personality or social disorder. Boys generally enter a stage in early adolescence in which homosexual acts occur that range from mutual masturbation to actual physical sexual acts with each other. This period of early adolescence may be marked by increased "gang" and male group identification. Social interaction, belonging, and intimate relationships provide the opportunity to practice bonds of trust and mutuality with another human being. Girls also experience a period in which they spend much of their time with other girls. However, both sexes, as they mature into middle and late adolescence, usually transfer this mutuality and affection to members of the opposite sex.

126

The adolescent hustler who performs homosexual acts with known homosexual adults usually does not see himself as a homosexual, because he differentitates between homosexual acts and homosexuality. To the hustler, homosexuals are individuals who "do it for free because they enjoy it" rather than for money. The true homosexual is an individual who continues to find more satisfaction in relationships with men than in those with the opposite sex. He seeks pairing relationships with other men as heterosexual men do with women.

As with prostitution, there are adjusted homosexuals and maladjusted homosexuals. The individual who, because of individual factors, including hormonal and genetic factors, environment and learning, and personality characteristics, chooses to become a homosexual may be as well adjusted to his life style as is the heterosexual man or woman. In a homosexual pair, one partner may assume the male role and the other the female role. These roles are given a variety of names that imply the individual sexuality of each partner. Some homosexuals find both heterosexual and homosexual experiences satisfying but prefer homosexual relationships as continuing or permanent relationships.

Frequently, when homosexual men or women reach middle age, they display a declining interest in the physical sexual aspects of their relationships, as do heterosexual individuals. At this point in their lives, they may appear less homosexual to others and adjust within the community much like other single or married individuals.

The individual who has definite psychological leanings toward homosexuality during adolescence often struggles for several years with much internal emotional conflict and may develop long-lasting personality difficulties. Many adolescents, desiring to be accepted and admired by their peers, often have some fears of being homosexual. Homosexuality can be a much dreaded behavior in adolescent "gangs," since the members draw from the group feelings of "manhood" and male identity. Since each individual in such a group is there in order to be accepted and identified as a competent male, the group's behavior toward known adult or adolescent homosexuals can be quite violent. Each member's identity and sense of his maleness are threatened by such individuals. For the adolescent struggling with an emerging awareness of homosexual leanings, the effects of gang membership can cause severe depression and anxiety. In some cases, individual adolescents with strong homosexual tendencies develop what is called, in psychological terms, a *reaction formation*. The reaction formation involves an individual's attempt to react strongly in a direction opposite to repressed feelings and tendencies. Such an individual may become overly concerned about demonstrating his manhood through severe criminality or other behavior that proves how tough he is. The conquest of women, brutality toward others, and

127

gang leadership roles become important in controlling his latent tendencies toward homosexuality. Such compensation may propel the individual into continual confrontation with the law. Such an individual is disturbed and an example of a "maladjusted" homosexual. Rehabilitation would be very difficult but would most likely be accomplished through assisting him in accepting his own sexuality rather than "normal" heterosexuality.

There are many so-called closet homosexuals in the middle class who are married, hold responsible positions, and have a more or less adequate family life. In some cases, these individuals eventually "come out of the closet," that is, become overt homosexuals later in life. Others maintain their secret and have affairs with other homosexuals whom they may meet in the office, factory, or other locations, including bus stations and singles' or "gay" bars, or through fraternal and social organizations.

It is during adolescence that many boys and girls first begin to struggle with the problem of their sexuality. Because of the tendency of adolescent groups and gangs to reinforce male and female stereotypes, this can be a period of intense personal crisis. This can result in either personality disorders or extreme criminality as a means of dealing with the internal struggle to establish an appropriate personal identity.

DRUG ABUSE

The use and misuse of drugs by adolescents is no less a tangle of values and issues than any of the other problems of adolescence. Drug programs and other attempts to deal with the "drug problem" during adolescence have generally failed. Public reaction has subsided, and there is less furor in recent years than in the early 1970's; however, drug misuse by adolescents is no less serious today than in the early 1970's. It has merely returned to its original role of a somewhat hidden and even societally repressed problem. The public seems to be unable to maintain its interest in any one social problem for an extended period of time. The nature of drug abuse has changed somewhat, but it continues to be a significant problem to schools, to parents of children in school, and to law enforcement agencies.

The hallmark of adolescence is the individual's emergence as an autonomous person looking for a place and an identity. He or she needs to be accepted by peers and needs time to engage in pseudoadult activities without the constraints and taboos of true adulthood, which requires personal and family responsibility and productivity. Adolescence is a time of play at being an adult and of finding one's self. Feelings abound in the adolescent, and he or she seeks to heighten them, to express them, to share them, and to understand their meaning. The adolescent of today is a much more sophisticated and socially aware individual than his older brothers and sisters were as adolescents in the 1960's. He knows about drugs, the issues and problems associated with drugs, and the varying attitudes and beliefs held concerning drugs. Marijuana has become, in both the middle class and the subcultures, an accepted tool to increase social interaction and enhance intimate stimulation. The use of other drugs, including heroin, LSD, cocaine, amphetamines, and PCP, is widespread and probably more so than in the past. Alcohol has again become a favorite in certain groups of adolescents, as it was in their parents' youth. Drugs, money to buy them, and the opportunity to engage in drug use without detection and arrest all contribute to the current existence of a large drug market in this country, although the public seems to be somewhat unaware of the problem.

The adolescent culture of today includes moderate and restricted use of drugs, particularly marijuana, at parties, on dates, and at school. Often, marijuana is used to gain a mild high to help one through the dullness of the day or to enhance the effects of music and social interaction at parties. There are social rules and behaviors that the adolescent group establishes attached to the use of the milder drugs. The use of drugs often is intended to enhance social activity, and the users remain aware and responsible for their behavior.

The adolescent, contrary to popular belief, is not introduced into the drug culture by a "dope peddler" but by a friend, a roommate, a girlfriend or boyfriend, or other adolescents. The effects of various drugs are not always immediately recognized by the individual; he or she actually has to "learn" not only how to use the drug but also to recognize and enjoy its effects. The tingling skin, mild euphoria, dizziness, and other effects of the drug are usually frightening to the initiate, and he may not expect or be able to successfully deal with the effects unless he is assisted by someone who is experienced. Usually, the motivation for drug use is social acceptance, intimacy or status, that is, the needs of the normal adolescent.

Drug use symbolizes friendship and sharing. The mutual high that the adolescent experiences from the drug enhances his or her feeling of intimacy with and acceptance by friends, like the rituals of primitive tribes of South America, the peace pipe of the American Indians, and even the social rituals of today's adult culture. The drug provides enhanced personal awareness, and a feeling of wholeness is gained as part of group rituals concerning initiation into a brotherhood.

Thus, in the beginning, drug use is part of a complex matrix of behavior involving the essentials of social behavior and acceptance by others. Even in adolescent gangs in urban areas, drug use is usually controlled and defined by the mores of the group. However, drug users can become addicts; the addict may become criminal in order to satisfy

129

his habit. The addict often uses hard drugs and takes them intravenously. Tolerance is built up quickly at first and more slowly later on. The addict does not seem to experience the high of the occasional user; with its enhanced social activity and feelings of intimacy. He takes the drug to satisfy his habit and to avoid the now certain consequences of not taking it. Contrary to popular belief, the addict does not necessarily enjoy the effects of the drug. The addict appears to be an individual who is acting out avoidance behavior rather than seeking enhancement of self. The dread of withdrawal symptoms spurs the addict on in his habit, which requires ever greater funds and time and thus makes it impossible for him to hold down a job or engage in normal social activities. His time must be spent in obtaining the drug. Few addicts have more than a few hours' or a day's supply and are therefore constantly in search of the drug or of money to buy it.

Many studies have been done of the personalities of drug addicts and alcoholics; however, it has been difficult to distinguish any special personality characteristics that identify the drug user or alcoholic. Popular psychological literature has often conveyed the image of the downtrodden or neurotic individual who is attempting to escape himself and his failures as the prototype of the addict. Other studies point to more severe personality disturbances in such individuals; however, it is difficult to know whether the individuals in these particular studies are actually representative of the culture. Drug addiction and alcoholism are complex issues involving transitory situations, personality, social and family history, and opportunity. It is difficult to establish that any particular socioeconomic or occupational group or personality type is more prone to addiction or alcoholism.

In today's society, the police officer must play a critical role in dealing with drug problems, as in many other areas of dealing with adolescents. He is often caught between the laws and the expectation of the public that he will enforce them, despite the fact that arrest and detention are not necessarily appropriate in most cases. If officers arrested and detained all traffic offenders and all adolescent groups that become a nuisance, the courts would never be able to manage them. Similarly, if police officers arrested every teenager who they knew had been using marijuana, the courts would also be flooded beyond hope of ever processing all the cases. Even when adolescents are arrested and do go to court, a great number are not sentenced to detention in a correctional institution.

The officer must look at the situation in the context of the particular instance of violation to decide what action should be taken. Selective enforcement is a reality in police work and serves a critical social function, although, according to their legal mandate, it is unacceptable. Furthermore, the police officer in a precinct or county district must sometimes give an adolescent his freedom in exchange for information so that the "supplier" can be apprehended rather than the user. Many complications can arise in this type of enforcement: a detailed investigation and the building of evidence toward the arrest of a ring of suppliers may be interrupted when users are arrested by policemen not aware of or involved in the investigation.

SUICIDE

The incidence of suicide during adolescence varies to some degree according to geographic location, cultural group, and other factors, but, in general, it is less common among the lower socioeconomic classes and more common in the middle class. There may be a relationship between intelligence or language level and potential for suicide, since it is more prevalent among adolescents who are not from impoverished homes or rejecting, economically deprived, or brutal homes.

According to Durkheim,[6] there are three major types of suicide: altruistic, egoistic, and anomic. Altruistic suicide is usually confined to special cultural or group situations and involves taking one's life for the good of the group. The old, the physically handicapped, or individuals who feel they are in some way a burden to the group may commit this type of suicide; situations in war are also characteristic of this form of suicide. Egoistic suicide may result when an individual feels alienated from others or in some way lost and unable to find reason to live. Anomic suicide involves a feeling of loss or value, as when an individual is faced with the confusion or breakdown of the values of his society or group.

The incidence of suicide and attempted suicide among adolescents is generally overstated, probably because of the tragedy of one so young taking his life. Most studies indicate that adolescence is one of the lowest incidence groups. There often seem to be few objective reasons for the suicide of an adolescent. However, it should be remembered that adolescence is not usually characterized by rational behavior, that is, not before the formation of a personal identity. An understanding of the current theory of suicide may shed some light on the subject of adolescent suicide.

The suicide process appears to involve a search for the resolution of self-perceived problems that finally ends with the choice of suicide. There is usually a history of unresolved problems. Frequently, an escalation of these problems occurs at a particular time for the individual. The individual continues to fail to develop techniques to deal with his problems; a period follows when the individual feels he has experienced an abrupt and unanticipated dissolution of meaningful relationships. He feels that there is no hope and no one to assist him in his dilemma.

131

Often the suicidal individual reaches a stage where his own death becomes almost an obsession and is a *dominant* theme of his life pattern. Once the individual chooses suicide, there is a *fixation* involved, which means that he can no longer select any alternative. There is an increasing *lack of objectivity* combined with an *interpretation of the problem that precludes any solution.*

Paralleling these formulations by sociologists of the final stages of the suicide process is a cognitive theory of mental process that further explains the problem. Individuals faced with important decisions, as perceived by themselves, enter a stage of mental process called *cognitive dissonance.* We have often seen this process in a variety of individuals who are facing personal crises or attempting to alter their lives in some major way. The process involves first recognizing and defining a specific goal. In this case, suicide becomes a possible goal. Once the individual rules out the alternatives, he still must *convince* himself that this is the appropriate decision. Although this is the decision the indivdiual has reached, it will not simply be acted on but requires a period of testing and evaluation. The individual must now "rationally" work out a sound basis for accepting the goal. This process demonstrates that most individuals who commit suicide are not "out of their minds" or in a temporary state of emotional disturbance or psychosis. In fact, they very carefully consider the reasons why suicide is the most logical goal. In this stage, the individual is slowly resolving any "dissonance" he has about his decision. He may talk to others in a theoretical way about suicide, read materials about the process, and consider various cultural and historical examples of suicide. As he investigates suicide, he will slowly convince himself of why it is the best solution. He slowly resolves internal dissonance and at some point is satisfied that this is the best course. He has resolved his cognitive dissonance, and suicide is imminent.

Often individuals who call prevention centers or a trusted friend are in the final stages of resolving their cognitive dissonance. This is why they often talk at length, waiting for the other person to give them reasons that they can test against their own emerging belief. There is an internal need to solve a problem, and because the individual has tentatively selected suicide, he has a tendency to argue with the person he has called. This is an example of the attempt to resolve cognitive dissonance; at this point, the friend or suicide prevention personnel can have the most effect. The suicidal individual can be led backward toward solutions he had not thought of, back past the point of cognitive dissonance about his intended goal to the consideration of preceding goals. If prevention personnel can do this, they can move the individual away from suicide; however, this is often a difficult task and requires much training.

For individuals in a developmental stage where intense emotions exist, contemplation of suicide is common. However, parents, friends, or teachers may inadvertently offer the individual a meaningful relationship, a solution to their problem, or assistance in understanding it in more realistic terms. The counselor may not be aware that the individual is contemplating suicide and yet actually prevent it. This is why an understanding of the adolescent state is so important to all adults who work with adolescents. Frequently, the problems that precipitate suicide in the adolescent are trivial problems to the adult. At a critical stage of the adolescent's life, however, such problems can be life shattering. This emphasizes how important the development of a new self-identity, the establishment of a social role, and the resolution of discontinuity can be to the adolescent. Of those adolescents who contemplate suicide, few actually follow through, but the signs of depression, withdrawal, change of usual habits, and continuing periods of intense unrest and personal concern are often quite evident if there is anyone to see them. This is why the impersonal nature of the schools, the lack of parental concern and attention, and the general problems of peer relationships can often be the stimulants to unfortunate suicides by seemingly normal adolescents.

It seems unbelievable that police officers, teachers, parents, and pastoral personnel have so little training or true understanding of the many adolescents who are their responsibility. Few of these individuals are aware of the processes and problems that occur in adolescence. Most adolescent suicides are related to the unavailability of adults and friends who can give adolescents the friendship, time, and support they need to get through a period of life that is the final stage in becoming an adult human being. It is surprising that there are not more suicides rather than less during this period of exceptional change and growth.

ASSAULT ON THE SCHOOL

Teachers are raped, knifed, battered, threatened, ridiculed, defied, and damned by individual adolescents and gangs of adolescents. Violence in schools has been traditionally a ghetto or urban problem but is spreading to suburban and rural schools, to middle-class schools and upper-class schools. Schools are designed to educate and socialize the young; in many of today's schools, the essential conflict is between the autonomy of the adolescent and the authority of the school. Schools are being sued for violation of individual rights and forced to desegregate. Special interest groups are forcing, through legislative action, curriculum changes, and an increasingly large portion of school budgets is going not only to salaries and maintenance but to security and repairs necessary because of vandalism. Parents in all economic groups are blaming the schools for the liberalism and falling level of achievement of their children and for a variety of social ills that have increased the number of qualifications necessary to the adolescent in the employment marketplace. There seems to be no relief in sight for the social and economic woes of the ever-growing secondary schools. The problems are those of society and not the schools. The schools are society's institutions, however, and demands for change are rampant. The liberalizing curriculum and programming changes instituted in the 1960's and early 1970's have not worked.

Why does the adolescent go to school, if not for an education? He goes because that is where his friends are and where the action is. Today's secondary schools, despite the demands placed on them by society, are better equipped and better organized and operated than they ever have been. The teachers are more effectively trained in subject matter, and the entire system of secondary education is probably more effective than it has ever been. However, the system is failing to meet the needs of the ever-increasing numbers of adolescents in preparing them for adulthood and living in a complex technological society. The schools are still too traditional and inflexible and are unable to provide the kinds of training and services demanded by our culture. For many of the adolescents, the end of the road is the law enforcement officer and state correctional institutions or facilities. That most adolescents make it through high school demonstrates their own determination rather than the effectiveness of the school. However, one must ask, in all fairness to the secondary school: Can our present system of education and educational philosophy truly meet the needs of today's society, or are we asking more than can be given? Is there a need for an alternate system of education to supplement the old? The answer is probably *yes,* but who will be willing to pay for it? At what cost? The power groups and economic groups who are the most verbal in effecting change in schools may also be the groups least concerned about needy students. Who will speak for the Blacks, the Chicanos, and the migrant workers and transitory families? Who will speak for the rights of girls to a newer and more broadly based curriculum, and who will speak for the desperate students for whom school is only a temporary refuge from the street? These questions must be answered if we are to meet the educational needs of more children.

When an adolescent is alienated from the usual peer group culture, several factors may affect his or her problematic interaction with the school. For much of the peer group culture, high school is an experience that will prepare them for college or the work world of adulthood. For the alienated student, however, the following factors prevent its being this kind of experience:

1. The alienated student often has a history of poor school achievement and attitudes that prevent adjustment.
2. The alienated student has not developed the academic skills needed for achievement in high school.
3. The alienated student can find acceptance only in "out" groups, thus increasing his alienation through gang membership.
4. The school curriculum is designed primarily for the middle-class student and relies on attendant social values and parental attitudes that reinforce achievement.
5. The mode of dress of deprived or alienated students causes negative expectations by teachers, thus further alienating the student.
6. Teachers often see their relationship to students as one of "teachers" to "learners," rather than one of socialization and interpersonal responsibility, of attempting to "reach" and assist the student.
7. Teachers too often are unwilling to spend the additional time needed to assist the underachieving student or the student with personal problems.
8. The increased size of secondary schools makes teachers, by necessity managing large groups, impersonal and inaccessible to the student with special needs.
9. The alienated student often gets little assistance from guidance counselors, who, like the teachers, tend to discriminate against problem students. They spend more time in schedule counseling, and their time is not available for the sort of counseling needed by many students.
10. The dean of men or women is more often an administrative assistant or an in-house policeman than a facilitator between teachers, students, and the curriculum.
11. The parents of alienated students are often the last to come to school, the least likely to take part in parent-school groups, and the most difficult to contact concerning their children's needs.
12. There is little relationship or communication between community agencies, law enforcement agencies, and mental health agencies that must deal with adolescents who need special help.
13. Communication and the division of responsibilities between the school and community agencies are poor or nonexistent, and their services often work against each other and the adolescent.
14. For the alienated youth, crime, status offenses, and street culture are often more reliable socializers and teachers than school.
15. There are few occupational training or alternative school programs across the country that are designed for the marginal student or the student with limited resources or educational goals.

135

The most that many teachers can do for such youth is to attempt to prevent conflict and to maintain a marginal authority for themselves and a degree of autonomy for the student. Education and learning are secondary goals to maintaining order and avoiding violence and confrontation until the student passes from view, either by graduating or going to jail.

Surprisingly, the school appears insulated from street hustles, adolescent prostitution, homosexual prostitution, status offenses, and the many other forms of adolescent crime and social confrontation that occur daily and nightly around the neighborhood. By day, the student walking into the school is expected to join the joyful ranks of other students anxious to learn and seek the good life. Surprisingly also, many alienated students pull it off, with a little bit of turning the head by the teacher, and peace prevails . . . for a while. The teacher learns to not push the student and to let him sleep, miss class, and maintain some degree of personal autonomy, while the student allows the teacher to play the role of authority and even complies with many of his demands. Both learn how to subtly give each other room to move without seriously confronting or challenging the other or asking more than he is willing to give. World governments would be proud of this diplomatic compromise, this exercise of elementary animal avoidance of aggression. Occasionally, however, one makes a wrong move, and coalitions form and the challenge is set; the teacher and the student become involved in a game of intimidation and threat that usually stops just short of outright conflict. At any time, however, one or the other may attempt to exercise authority over the other despite the nonverbal truce, and violence follows. This is not an unusual relationship. The student indicates to the teacher that he needs room to maneuver, that he will comply with classroom authority if it is recognized that he is complying and not submitting, as long as the teacher allows him his autonomy and choice. The teacher, in exchange for granting this autonomy, is able to exercise certain prerogatives of authority. The teacher can request that the student be quiet, not disrupt the class, display at least passing interest, and complete just enough work to give the impression that he is learning. The teacher passes the student with a marginal grade, high enough for eventual graduation, and breathes a sigh of relief that he is gone. This subtle agreement of autonomy and authority between teacher and student is a delicate relationship that tends to constantly approach minor confrontation that can result in conflict. Usually, as in all good diplomacy, one or both parties utilize verbal threats, intimidation through gestures, and withdrawal, before reaching a temporary truce and reestablishing their delicate agreement.

This kind of agreement is often developed not only in a particular teacher's class but in many of the student's classes. It is usually an occasion for much joy when such a student is picked up by the local police and moved on his way to some sort of correctional program. Frequently, the student is part of an adolescent gang that roams the community at night and provides the adolescent with membership in a kind of family. He is often caught in the group and could not leave it even if he wanted to. The adolescent group provides the focus of his life, and even here he plays the game of autonomy and authority, but with peers. He struggles for a place somewhere and joins in the crimes and confrontations that are part of gang life. He engages in the challenge of one gang to another, as he does in the challenge to teachers and parents.

The gang may be a somewhat cohesive group of individuals who protect each other. They set standards and rules for behavior in the streets in order to effectively perpetrate crimes for money and thrills. The gang provides a degree of acceptance and companionship. However, the adolescent may, as is more often the case, be in a group that is disorganized and provides only a place to go to find "action," that almost by accident gets into trouble with the law, and that continues more as a collection of individuals than as an organized and effective group that can give him a feeling of belonging.

As an individual, odd as it may seem, he may often look forward to someday having a good job and a family like anyone else. Leaving, or deserting, the group will be difficult. One of the few ways to leave such a group is through marriage, which symbolizes that he has become an adult and no longer qualifies for gang membership.

This is the individual who sits in the classroom. He is unable to become "straight" even if he wanted to. In fleeting moments when a teacher does reach him, he may want to finally make peace and join the world as a responsible person, but he cannot. The school is unable to reach these adolescents, and we can see that the problems go beyond the realm of the school's responsibility. New curricula and new social programs will not be enough. Community action programs in cooperation with the school are necessary.

REFERENCES

1. Kobetz, R. W. *The police role and juvenile delinquency.* Gaithersburg, Md.: International Association of Police Chiefs, 1971.
2. Thompson, B. *Child abuse and neglect: A school-community resource book.* Madison, Wis.: Wisconsin Department of Public Instruction, Bulletin No. 9096, 1977, pp. 104, 106.
3. Burgess, A., & Holmstrom, L. Rape trauma syndrome. *American Journal of Psychiatry,* 1974, *131,* 981-986.
4. Bohmer, C. Judicial attitudes toward rape victims. *Judicature,* 1974, *57,* 303-307.
5. Keefe, M. L., & O'Reilly, H. T. Changing perspectives in sex crimes. In M. J. Walker & S. L. Brodsky (Eds.), *Sexual assault.* Lexington, Mass.: D. C. Heath, 1976, p. 161.

6. Durkheim, E. *Suicide* (J. A. Spalding & G. Simpson, trans.). Glencoe, Ill.: The Free Press, 1951.

ADDITIONAL READINGS

Adler, F. *Sisters in crime.* New York: McGraw-Hill, 1975.

Brodsky, A. *The female offender.* Beverly Hills, Calif.: Sage, 1975.

Clinard, M. B. *Sociology of deviant behavior.* New York: Holt, Rinehart & Winston, 1974.

Coffey, A., Eldefonso, E., & Hartinger, W. *Human relations: Law enforcement in a changing community.* Englewood Cliffs, N.J.: Prentice-Hall, 1976.

Cohn, A., & Viano, E. *Police community relations: Images, roles, realities.* Philadelphia: J. B. Lippincott, 1976.

Gebhard, P., Ganon, J., Pomeroy, W., & Christenson, C. *Sex offenders.* New York: Harper & Row, 1965.

Reckless, W. C. *American criminology: New directions.* New York: Appleton-Century-Crofts, 1973.

Simon, R. J. *Women and crime.* Lexington, Mass.: Lexington Books, 1975.

CHAPTER 8

A FINAL STATEMENT

My shadow casts itself before the sun,
Who shall I be, and when?

Our discussions here concerning adolescence have been brief and often little more than a suggestion of the scope of the problems and issues that confront and confound the adolescent and adults who must deal with adolescents at home, on the streets, and in school. However, the discussions have been aimed at the police officer, who in many cases has little knowledge of adolescence beyond his or her own experience. Ashburn pointed out the unavailability of training that would provide the basis for the development of a true "professional" status for the police officer.[1] Although police work is generally considered a profession, the roles and training of police officers are still widely divergent from community to community throughout the country. Much of the information available to the police officer deals with law enforcement, whereas much less is provided in psychology, sociology, and other areas that will be important in the coming years to effectively perform the challenging role of law enforcement.

The following themes from our discussions may provide a basis for understanding adolescents and the crimes they commit:

1. Adolescence is a period of personal growth that, because of its nature, has moments in which the normal individual may find it difficult to maintain appropriate and law-abiding behavior. Thus, the nature of adolescence itself may contribute to confrontation between the adolescent and society.
2. Many adolescents experience transitory periods of emotional difficulty that stimulate episodes of delinquent behavior, whereas other adolescents are in fact delinquent because of long-term personality and social disorders.
3. Many adolescents from cultural subgroups, because of the social and cultural nature of their environment, are prone to delinquent and criminal behavior as a consequence of limited opportunities and choices.
4. National emphasis on the changing attitude toward women's roles is affecting the incidence of reported crime among adolescent girls.
5. The police role is becoming more complex; however, training too often is limited to enforcement strategies instead of being "professional" training stressing the nature of criminality rather than its existence and prevention.

Our discussions have focused on issues of normal adolescence with emphasis on delinquency and law enforcement. Because of the focus on adolescence itself, many problems of delinquency have gone unmentioned. However, an introduction to these problems aimed at the beginning police officer is necessarily limited. Lists of additional readings have been provided for police trainers and officers who wish to investigate in more depth any of the areas discussed. We leave it to the officer himself to take the initiative after reading our overview. The following major issues should be kept in mind when formulating and developing training programs for police officers in the field of juvenile problems.

MAJOR AREAS OF CONCERN IN ADOLESCENCE

The central concerns of the adolescent, regardless of socioeconomic or geographic factors, include the development of a personal and group identity, resolution of discontinuity, and eventual establishment of feelings of worth, autonomy, and competency. Personal growth is the goal of adolescence that provides the fuel for the many problems related to adolescence, including adolescent delinquency. The task of social agencies and law enforcement personnel to assist youth who fail to establish such identity is so complex and demanding that we often fail, and the adolescent struggles to adjust or not on his own.

THE DIVERGENT ISSUES OF MIDDLE-CLASS AND LOWER-CLASS DELINQUENCY

Delinquency has most frequently been identified by the public in relation to the poor, the disadvantaged, and the poorly educated. Few writers on sociology or criminal justice fail to point out the inqualities in treatment between the poor and the affluent. For the police officer, understanding the sociological and personality differences between the poor and the affluent is itself a monumental task. Even more difficult are the conflicts the officer feels as a consequence of his own perception of the individual he meets on the street. Goldman pointed out how differential treatment of juveniles by police officers can be related to a number of factors, including race, sex, economic background, nature of offense, and geographic region.[2]

THE CHANGING ROLE OF WOMEN AND THEIR CRIMES

It is difficult to read an article, a pamphlet, or a book today that attempts to explain the increasing role of women in crime without finding that it contradicts another source. Some authors stress the increase in criminal involvement of women and girls in recent years: an increase of 306% for adolescent girls between 1960 and 1972 compared with an increase for adolescent boys of 82% during the same period. Others point out that women are not necessarily committing more crimes but are being arrested more frequently than in the past.[3]

The liberation of women has not only brought more criminality among women to light; there is also an increase in criminality, violence, and acceptance of a traditionally male role among adolescent girls. Violent gangs of adolescent girls, with no association with groups of boys,

141

are emerging, in addition to female branches of male delinquent gangs. Sociologists and psychologists are busily involved in an attempt to explain, describe, and analyze what is, or seems to be, happening. The police officer and the correctional worker are finding that there is an increase in crimes by adolescent girls and that these crimes are more often crimes traditionally committed by boys and men. Assessment of the problem is further clouded by current trends toward conservatism in many parts of the culture, with a return to more traditional patterns of male and female behavior, combined with the continuing escalation of aggressiveness and criminality among adolescent girls in other socioeconomic groups. Many dimensions of the sociological structure are difficult to specify. The officer must deal with what *is* rather than with what may be or why it may be. However, in the coming years there will certainly be greater divergence in sexual roles due to a strengthening of traditional sexual stereotypes in some groups and a weakening of the stereotypes in others. This will complicate both understanding of and intervention in adolescent crime. In this area, both police training and law enforcement agency–community relationships will have to be greatly improved, with new programs and services for both police officers and the community.

In summary, we suggest that the national trend at this time in the behavior of women is not for them to become more like men but to engage in more aggressive acts associated with male stereotypes. The behavior and the motivation may not be the same. Furthermore, the more aggressive crimes are still being committed by members of subcultural groups. In an interesting study completed by Panton, a personality test was used to analyze the personality structure of 128 male inmates and 128 female inmates of a state penal institution.[4] This fairly recent study suggested several important personality differences between male and female inmates:

1. The mean profile of the female inmates was significantly less deviant than that of the male inmates. The male inmates were far more characterized by overconcern with physical functioning and by poor morale, voiced pessimism, emotional immaturity, and irritability. The female inmates exhibited more oversubjectivity and oversensitivity and a greater inclination to avoid establishing meaningful relationships.
2. The male inmates scored higher on scales associated with overt conflict with authority and the female inmates higher on scales reflecting feelings of isolation and a lack of pleasure in social intercourse.
3. The male inmates generally presented a more sociopathic profile, whereas the female inmates were more asocial than antisocial.

4. These results compared significantly with those of an earlier study (Hathaway and Monchesi, 1969; cited by Brodsky, 1975) that was done with adolescent girls.[4]

Much of the literature on the increasing violence and "masculine" behavior of adolescent girls, both on the streets and in correctional institutions, does not indicate that women are more violent because they are liberated but that they may be more violent than is *expected for women.* Both men and women are capable of violence, but it does not necessarily follow that the basic nature of the female personality is changing. This demonstrates how biased our expectations and beliefs about women have always been in a male-dominated culture. Women in prison today may be more violent than men in general, and there may be a greater number of women in some prisons than in the past. However, it is probable that women are expressing frustration and anger openly now, whereas men continue to adopt a more generalized aggressiveness as part of their nature. Violence as the reaction of a woman to containment and authority is no different from violence as the reaction of a man. However, men continue to be more aggressive in their general nature.

The important point for police officers and correctional personnel is that the motivations to violence in women and men will probably continue to represent the differences in sexual stereotypes. We believe that police officers will continue to find more threat of violence in the general population of men than in the population of women in the coming years. Only time will bear us out or prove us wrong. Most officers on the street will know the answer before the sociologist.

THE NEED FOR DRASTIC ALTERATION IN OUR EDUCATIONAL SYSTEM

The schools remain a major deterrent or stimulant to the problems of adolescence and delinquency. There are indications in today's schools of a return to a more depersonalized and rigid standard of behavior and academic structure. The schools stand as a major socializing institution between the family and society. The role of law enforcement officers is not that of educators and parents. If changes in the rate of crime and delinquency are to occur, society will have to provide the vehicle for change. The law enforcement agency is presently in the position of solving problems that it is in the worst position to affect.

Our schools are not meeting the needs of the adolescent who becomes delinquent any better than his family. The complications of communication in interagency programs between the legal system and the schools are no less today than 20 years ago and perhaps greater. Unless increased effectiveness in this area is realized, there is no hope that the courts can in some way solve the problem. Who should take the first step? Adoles-

143

cence is here to stay. We hope that this short confrontation with adolescence will help the police officer to develop his professional role toward one of greater effectiveness in assisting the juvenile delinquent and to develop new and more effective ways of communicating to the schools and state legislatures the basic issues involved.

REFERENCES

1. Ashburn, F. G. Changing the rhetoric of "professionalism." *Innovation in law enforcement.* Washington, D.C.: U.S. Department of Justice, Law Enforcement Assistance Administration, National Institute of Law Enforcement and Criminal Justice, 1973, pp. 1-11.
2. Goldman, N. *The differential selection of juvenile offenders for court appearance.* Washington, D.C.: National Research and Information Center, NCDD, 1963, pp. 25-30; 125-133.
3. Pollak, O. *The criminality of women.* Philadelphia: University of Pennsylvania Press, 1950.
4. Panton, J. Personality differences between male and female inmates measured by the MMPI. In A. Brodsky, *The female offender.* Beverly Hills, Calif.: Sage, 1975.

INDEX

145